WELCOME

Thanks for purchasing these training notes for the **AWS Certified Cloud Practitioner** exam from Digital Cloud Training. The information in these Cheat Sheets relates to the latest version of the **CLF-C01** version of the exam blueprint.

The aim of putting this information together is to provide a centralized, detailed list of the facts you need to know before you sit the exam. This will shortcut your study time and maximize your chance of passing the AWS Certified Cloud Practitioner exam first time.

I hope you get great value from this popular resource that has been well received by our pool of over 250,000 students.

Wishing you all the best for your AWS Certified Cloud Practitioner Associate exam.

Neal Davis

Neal Davis

Founder of Digital Cloud Training

DigitalCloud
TRAINING

WHAT DO OTHER STUDENTS SAY?

Check out the excellent reviews from our many students who passed their AWS exam with an average passing score of over 850!

If I had only known how valuable this book would be, I would've bought this and saved a lot of time and money spent on other sources of AWS study materials. This book provides the AWS Cloud Practitioner Exam content in an organized, easier to understand format for us novice cloudies. Highly recommend.

I enjoyed the book; it was an easy read and a great way to prepare for the Cloud Practitioner exam. Neal Davis explains the concepts clearly, includes great visuals and practice questions. The purchase also gives you the ability to create a Digital Cloud account which provides additional resources (free and paid) including more notes and practice questions and exams.

A must-have study resource for the AWS Certified Cloud Practitioner CLF-C01 exam

TABLE OF CONTENTS

GETTING STARTED

ABOUT THESE TRAINING NOTES

Please note that this document does not read like a book or instructional text. We provide a raw, point-to-point list of facts backed by tables and diagrams to help with understanding.

For easy navigation, the information on each AWS service in this document is organized into the same categories as in the AWS Management Console.

The scope of coverage of services, and what information is included for each service, is based on feedback from our pool of over 250,000 students who have taken the exam, as well as our own experience - and may differ between AWS services.

To test your understanding, we have added **120 unique quiz questions** that you will find at the end of the major chapters. Please note that quiz questions are designed as a tool to review your knowledge of the content that was presented within the section. They do <u>not</u> necessarily represent the AWS exam style or difficulty. You will find examples of exam style practice questions within the chapter "How to best prepare for your exam".

YOUR PATHWAY TO SUCCESS

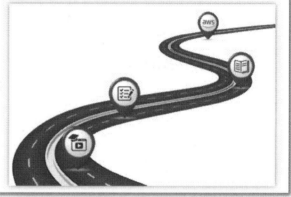

So, you're feeling excited to get started with the AWS Certified Cloud Practitioner certification and wondering what resources are out there to help you. Let's start with the free options. Visit https://digitalcloud.training/amazon-aws-free-certification-training-cloud-practitioner for links to various free resources including sample practice questions, blog articles, video tutorials and AWS documentation.

For the full training experience though, your best bet are the following training courses:

ON-DEMAND VIDEO COURSE

To get you started, we'd suggest first enrolling in the online instructor-led AWS Certified Cloud Practitioner Video Course from Digital Cloud Training to familiarize yourself with the AWS platform before returning to the Training Notes to get a more detailed understanding of the AWS services.

To learn more, visit https://digitalcloud.training/aws-certified-cloud-practitioner-training-course

Apply coupon code **AMZ20** at checkout for a **20% discount**.

PRACTICE EXAM COURSE

To assess where you are at on your AWS journey, we recommend taking the AWS Certified Cloud Practitioner Practice Exams on the Digital Cloud Training website. The **online exam simulator** with over **500 unique questions** will help you identify your strengths and weaknesses. These practice tests are designed to reflect the difficulty of the AWS exam and are the closest to the real exam experience available.

To learn more, visit https://digitalcloud.training/aws-certified-cloud-practitioner-practice-tests

Apply coupon code **AMZ20** at checkout for a **20% discount**.

Our online Practice Exams are delivered in 4 different variations:

- **Exam Mode**

  In exam simulation mode, you complete one full-length practice exam and answer all 65 questions within the allotted time. You are then presented with a pass / fail score report showing your overall score and performance in each knowledge area to identify your strengths and weaknesses.

- **Training Mode**

  When taking the practice exam in training mode, you will be shown the answers and explanations for every question after clicking "check". Upon completion of the exam, the score report will show your overall score and performance in each knowledge area.

- **Knowledge Reviews**

  Now that you have identified your strengths and weaknesses, you get to dive deep into specific areas with our knowledge reviews. You are presented with a series of questions focused on a specific topic. There is no time limit and you can view the answer to each question as you go through them.

- **Final Exam Simulator**

  The exam simulator randomly selects 65 questions from our pool of questions – mimicking the real AWS exam environment. The practice exam has the same format, style, time limit and passing score as the real AWS exam

TRAINING NOTES

As a final step, use these training notes to focus your study on the knowledge areas where you need to most. Get a detailed understanding of the AWS services and deep dive into the CLF-C01 exam objectives with detailed facts, tables and diagrams that will shortcut your time to success.

LIMITED TIME BONUS OFFER

To assess your AWS exam readiness, we have included one full-length practice exam from Digital Cloud Training with 65 exam-difficulty practice questions that are timed and scored and simulate the real AWS exam experience. To gain access to your free practice test on our interactive exam simulator online, simply navigate to the **CONCLUSION** at the back of this book where you'll find detailed instructions.

CONTACT, SUPPORT & FEEDBACK

We want you to get great value from these training resources. If for any reason you are not 100% satisfied, please contact us at support@digitalcloud.training. We promise to address all questions and concerns, typically within 24hrs. We really want you to have a 5-star learning experience!

The AWS platform is evolving quickly, and the exam tracks these changes with a typical lag of around 6 months. We are therefore reliant on student feedback to keep track of what is appearing in the exam. If there are any topics in your exam that weren't covered in our training resources, please provide us with feedback using this form https://digitalcloud.training/student-feedback/. We appreciate any feedback that will help us further improve our AWS training resources.

REVIEWS REALLY MATTER

If you enjoy reading reviews, please consider paying it forward. Reviews guide students and help us continuously improve our courses. We celebrate every honest review and truly appreciate it. We'd be thrilled if you could leave a rating at amazon.com/ryp or your local amazon store (e.g. amazon.co.uk/ryp).

JOIN THE AWS COMMUNITY

Our private Facebook group is a great place to ask questions and share knowledge and exam tips with the AWS community. Join the AWS Certification QA group on Facebook and share your exam feedback with the AWS community: https://www.facebook.com/groups/awscertificationqa

To join the discussion about all things related to Amazon Web Services on Slack, visit: http://digitalcloud.training/slack for instructions.

CONNECT WITH NEAL ON SOCIAL MEDIA

To learn more about the different ways of connecting with Neal, visit: https://digitalcloud.training/neal-davis

 digitalcloud.training/neal-davis

 youtube.com/c/digitalcloudtraining

facebook.com/digitalcloudtraining

 Twitter @nealkdavis

 linkedin.com/in/nealkdavis

 Instagram @digitalcloudtraining

HOW TO BEST PREPARE FOR YOUR EXAM

THE AWS EXAM BLUEPRINT

As a foundational level exam, the AWS Certified Cloud Practitioner is intended for individuals who have the ability to, in Amazon's words, "effectively demonstrate an overall understanding of the AWS Cloud". This certification is fairly generic and does not assess the skills required for specific job roles such as Developers, Sysops Administrators and Solutions Architects.

AWS recommend you have a minimum of 6 months experience with the AWS Cloud. However, this does not need to be experience in a technical job role. Exposure to the AWS Cloud in a managerial, sales, purchasing or financial position is also acceptable.

The exam includes 65 questions and has a time limit of 90 minutes. You need to score a minimum of 700 out of 1000 points to pass the exam.

The question format of the exam is multiple-choice (one correct response from four options) and multiple-response (two correct responses from five options).

As you'll see from the example questions later in this chapter, the questions are fairly straightforward and not scenario based like in other exams such as the Associate and Professional level certifications.

In the AWS Certified Cloud Practitioner exam blueprint, it is stated that **the exam validates an examinee's ability to**:

- Define what the AWS Cloud is and the basic global infrastructure
- Describe basic AWS Cloud architectural principles
- Describe the AWS Cloud value proposition
- Describe key services on the AWS platform and their common use cases (for example, compute and analytics)
- Describe basic security and compliance aspects of the AWS platform and the shared security model
- Define the billing, account management and pricing models
- Identify sources of documentation or technical assistance (for example, whitepapers or support tickets)
- Describe basic/core characteristics of deploying and operating in the AWS Cloud

Throughout the rest of this chapter, we'll explore these knowledge requirements in more detail, and will give you a clear idea of what to expect in the exam.

DOMAINS, OBJECTIVES AND EXAMPLES

The knowledge required is organized into four test "domains". Within each test domain there are several objectives that broadly describe the knowledge and experience expected to pass the exam.

Test Domain 1: Cloud Concepts

This domain makes up 28% of the exam and includes the following three objectives:

- 1.1 Define the AWS Cloud and its value proposition
- 1.2 Identify aspects of AWS Cloud economics
- 1.3 List the different cloud architecture design principles

What you need to know

You should be able to describe the benefits of public cloud services and be able to define what types of services are available on AWS (think IaaS, PaaS, SaaS). Make sure you understand the 6 advantages of cloud:

1. Trade capital expense for variable expense
2. Benefit from massive economies of scale
3. Stop guessing about capacity
4. Increase speed and agility
5. Stop spending money running and maintaining data centers
6. Go global in minutes

You need to know how cloud is beneficial from a financial perspective and should understand the difference between CAPEX and OPEX – this relates to item 1 in the list above.

You should understand the design principles of creating cloud architectures, this includes loose coupling, scaling (vertically and horizontally), bootstrapping and automation, to name just a few.

Example questions

Question: *Which feature of AWS allows you to deploy a new application for which the requirements may change over time?*

1. Elasticity
2. Fault tolerance
3. Disposable resources
4. High availability

Answer: 1, elasticity allows you to deploy your application without worrying about whether it will need more or less resources in the future. With elasticity, the infrastructure can scale on-demand

Question: *What advantages do you get from using the AWS cloud? (choose 2)*

1. Trade capital expense for variable expense
2. Stop guessing about capacity
3. Increased capital expenditure
4. Gain greater control of the infrastructure layer
5. Comply with all local security compliance programs

Answer: 1+2, with public cloud services such as AWS you can pay on a variable (OPEX) basis for the resources you use and scale on-demand, so you never need to guess how much resources you need to deploy.

Test Domain 2: Security

This domain makes up 24% of the exam and includes the following four objectives:

- 2.1 Define the AWS Shared Responsibility mode
- 2.2 Define AWS Cloud security and compliance concepts
- 2.3 Identify AWS access management capabilities
- 2.4 Identify resources for security support

What you need to know

You should understand the AWS shared responsibility model which defines who is responsible for different aspects of the technology stack from the data center through to servers, firewall rules and data encryption.

AWS provide tools and services for implementing security, assessing your security position, and generating alerts and compliance reports. You need to understand these services and tools well enough to describe their usage and benefits. This includes services such as KMS, CloudTrail and AWS Artifact.   *Audit*

You also need to understand the services that are used for authentication, authorization and access management. This includes services such as AWS IAM, and Amazon Cognito, and the usage of access keys, key pairs and signed URLs.

Support services include real-time insights through AWS Trusted Advisor and proactive support and advocacy with a Technical Account Manager (TAM). Make sure you know which support packages include a TAM.

Example questions

Question: *Under the AWS shared responsibility model what is the customer responsible for? (choose 2)*

1. Physical security of the data center
2. Replacement and disposal of disk drives
3. Configuration of security groups
4. Patch management of infrastructure
5. Encryption of customer data

Answer: 3+5, AWS are responsible for items such as the physical security of the DC, replacement of old disk drives, and patch management of the infrastructure whereas customers are responsible for items such as configuring security groups, network ACLs, patching their operating systems and encrypting their data.

Question: *Which AWS service is used to enable multi-factor authentication?*

1. Amazon STS
2. AWS IAM
3. Amazon EC2
4. AWS KMS

— G 662

Answer: 2, IAM is used to securely control individual and group access to AWS resources and can be used to manage multi-factor authentication.

Test Domain 3: Technology

This domain makes up 36% of the exam and includes the following four objectives:

- 3.1 Define methods of deploying and operating in the AWS Cloud
- 3.2 Define the AWS global infrastructure
- 3.3 Identify the core AWS services
- 3.4 Identify resources for technology support

What you need to know

You need to understand the core AWS services and what they are used for. You typically don't need a deep level of knowledge of the specifics of a service but do need to understand its purpose, benefits and use cases.

Core services include EC2, ECS, Lambda, LightSail, EBS, EFS, S3, RDS, DynamoDB, RedShift, ElastiCache, Elastic Load Balancing, Auto Scaling, CloudFront, Route 53, CloudWatch, CloudTrail, and SNS.

Monitoring   Audit

You should understand the underlying global infrastructure that makes up the AWS Cloud. This includes regions, availability zones, and edge locations. Make sure you understand which services are globally or regionally defined.

You should also know the customer configurable building blocks of cloud services including VPCs, and subnets, and connectivity options such as Internet Gateways, VPN and Direct Connect. Also, ensure you know the difference between NAT Instances and NAT Gateways and the relative benefits of each service.

Example questions

Question: *What are the advantages of Availability Zones? (choose 2)*

1. They allow regional disaster recovery
2. They provide fault isolation
3. They enable the caching of data for faster delivery to end users
4. They are connected by low-latency network connections
5. They enable you to connect your on-premises networks to AWS to form a hybrid cloud

Answer: 2+4, Each AWS region contains multiple distinct locations called Availability Zones (AZs). Each AZ is engineered to be isolated from failures in other AZs. An AZ is a data center, and in some cases, an AZ consists of multiple data centers. AZs within a region provide inexpensive, low-latency network connectivity to other zones in the same region. This allows you to replicate your data across data centers in a synchronous manner so that failover can be automated and be transparent for your users.

Question: *Which AWS support plans provide support via email, chat and phone? (choose 2)*

1. Basic
2. Business
3. Developer

4. Global

5. Enterprise

Answer: 2+5, only the business and enterprise plans provide support via email, chat and phone.

Test Domain 4: Billing and Pricing

This domain makes up 12% of the exam and includes the following three objectives:

- 4.1 Compare and contrast the various pricing models for AWS

- 4.2 Recognize the various account structures in relation to AWS billing and pricing

- 4.3 Identify resources available for billing support

What you need to know

Most services on AWS are offered on a pay per use basis, but there are also options to reduce price by locking in to 1- or 3-year contracts with various options for payment. You need to understand these models and which services they apply to.

Make sure you understand what AWS charges you for and what is free of charge. For instance, inbound data transfer is free whereas outbound data transfer typically incurs costs.

Some services such as VPC, CloudFormation, and IAM are free but the resources you create with them may not be. You need to understand where costs may be incurred.

AWS accounts can be organized into Organizations for centralized management of policies and consolidated billing. You need to understand the various accounts structures and the benefits and use cases for implementing them.

For instance, you might want separate account structures to manage different policies for production and non-production resources, or you might implement consolidated billing to take advantage of volume discounts.

For billing support, you need to know the services and tools available to you and what levels of support you can get from AWS support plans.

Tools include AWS Cost Explorer, AWS Simple Monthly Calculator, and Total Cost of Ownership (TCO) calculator.

Example questions

Question: *What are two ways an AWS customer can reduce their monthly spend? (choose 2)*

1. Turn off resources that are not being used

2. Use more power efficient instance types

3. Reserve capacity where suitable

4. Be efficient with usage of Security Groups

5. Reduce the amount of data ingress charges

Answer: 1+3, turning off resources that are not used can reduce spend. You can also use reserved instances to reduce the monthly spend at the expense of having to lock into a 1 or 3-year contract – good for stable workloads.

Question: *A company would like to maximize* their *potential volume and RI discounts across multiple accounts and also apply service control policies on member accounts. What can they use gain these benefits?*

1. AWS Budgets

2. AWS Cost Explorer

3. AWS IAM

4. AWS Organizations

Answer: 4, AWS Organizations enables you to create groups of AWS accounts and then centrally manage policies across those accounts. AWS Organizations provides consolidated billing in both feature sets, which allows you set up a single payment method in the organization's master account and still receive an invoice for individual activity in each member account. Volume pricing discounts can be applied to resources.

COMPUTE, STORAGE AND NETWORK CONCEPTS

This section provides a basic overview of some important compute, storage and networking concepts. It is aimed at those who are new to cloud computing or IT in general and not from a technical role.

Please note that the content within this section does not relate directly to the exam blueprint. It is foundational knowledge which will help you to understand some of the technical concepts that are presented later.

If you would like to skip this section and get straight to the content that relates to the exam blueprint, please go straight to section "Cloud Computing Concepts".

COMPUTE

INTRODUCTION TO COMPUTE

Along with storage and networking, compute is one of the key foundational building blocks of the cloud computing infrastructure layer. We will discuss the basic concepts you need to understand to get started with compute on AWS.

Fundamentally the term "compute" refers to physical servers comprised of the processing, memory, and storage required to run an operating system such as Microsoft Windows or Linux, and some virtualized networking capability.

The components of a compute server include the following:

- Processor or Central Processing Unit (CPU) - the CPU is the brains of the computer and carries out the instructions of computer programs

- Memory or Random Access Memory (RAM) - within a computer memory is very high speed storage for data stored on an integrated-circuit chip

- Storage - the storage location for the operating system files (and optionally data). This is typically a local disk stored within the computer or a network disk attached using a block protocol such as iSCSI

- Network - physical network interface cards (NICs) to support connectivity with other servers

When used in cloud computing, the operating system software that is installed directly on the server is generally a hypervisor which provides a hardware abstraction layer onto which additional operating systems can be run as virtual machines (VMs) or "instances". This technique is known as hardware virtualization.

A VM is a container within which virtualized resources including CPU (vCPU), memory and storage are presented, and an operating system can be installed. Each VM is isolated from other VMs running on the same host hardware and many VMs can run on a single physical host, with each potentially installed with different operating system software.

The diagram below depicts hardware virtualization with guest VMs running on top of a host OS:

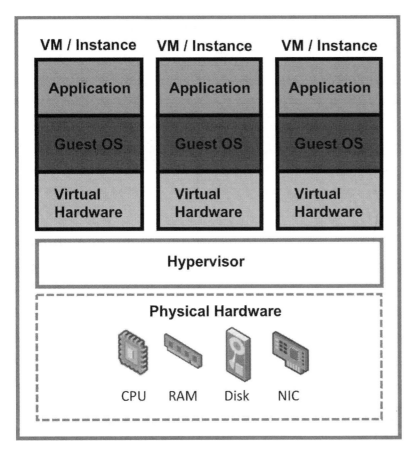

There are two main types of hypervisor:

- **Type 1** - the hypervisor is installed directly on top of the hardware and is considered a "bare-metal" hypervisor
- **Type 2** - the hypervisor software runs on top of a host operating system

Examples of Type 1 hypervisors include VMware ESXi and Microsoft Hyper-V and examples of Type 2 hypervisors include VMware Workstation and Oracle Virtual Box. Type 1 hypervisors typically provide better performance and security than Type 2 hypervisors.

While the diagram above shows a hardware virtualization stack using a Type 1 hypervisor, the diagram below depicts a Type 2 hypervisor:

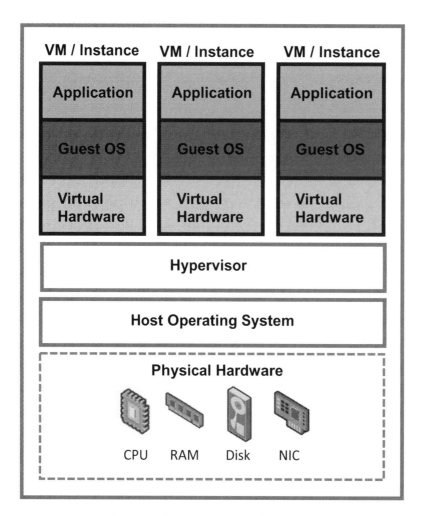

As you can see, the key difference is that a there is an additional host operating system layer that sits directly above the physical hardware and beneath the hypervisor layer.

Until recently, Amazon Web Services (AWS) used the Xen hypervisor but has now moved to an internally developed hypervisor based on the Kernel-based Virtual Machine (KVM) technology. KVM is generally considered to be a Type 1 hypervisor.

COMPUTE INSTANCES ON AWS

In AWS compute is consumed through the Elastic Compute Cloud (EC2) which is a web service from which you can launch "instances" which are essentially VMs running on the AWS KVM hypervisor.

Amazon EC2 provides secure, resizable compute capacity in the cloud on a pay-as-you-go basis with no fixed term contracts (unless you choose reserved instances to reduce cost).

There is a large selection of instance types you can choose from which come with varying specifications for vCPU, memory, and storage allocation.

Virtual networking is included with all instances and varies in performance level from low (unspecified performance) up to 25 Gigabit.

The image below shows a few "General Purpose" instance types. Note the different configurations for vCPU, Memory and Network Performance:

Family	Type	vCPUs (i)	Memory (GiB)	Instance Storage (GB) (i)	EBS-Optimized Available (i)	Network Performance (i)	IPv6 Support (i)
General purpose	t2.nano	1	0.5	EBS only	-	Low to Moderate	Yes
General purpose	t2.micro Free tier eligible	1	1	EBS only	-	Low to Moderate	Yes
General purpose	t2.small	1	2	EBS only	-	Low to Moderate	Yes
General purpose	t2.medium	2	4	EBS only	-	Low to Moderate	Yes
General purpose	t2.large	2	8	EBS only	-	Low to Moderate	Yes
General purpose	t2.xlarge	4	16	EBS only	-	Moderate	Yes
General purpose	t2.2xlarge	8	32	EBS only	-	Moderate	Yes
General purpose	t3.nano	2	0.5	EBS only	Yes	Up to 5 Gigabit	Yes

Instance types are categorized into families based on how the instance specifications are optimized for different usage scenarios. Optimizations that are available include compute, memory, storage, graphics processing (GPU) or general-purpose usage.

The following table shows the instance families currently available and describes the use cases they are best suited for:

Family	Hint	Purpose/Design
D	DATA	Heavy data usage (e.g. file servers, DWs)
R	RAM	Memory optimized
M	MAIN	General purpose (e.g. app servers)
C	COMPUTE	Compute optimized
G	GRAPHICS	Graphics intensive workloads
I	IOPS	Storage I/O optimised (e.g. NoSQL, DWs)
F	FAST	FPGA hardware acceleration for applications
T	CHEAP (think T2)	Lowest cost (e.g. T2–micro)
P	GPU	GPU requirements
X	EXTREME RAM	Heavy memory usage (e.g. SAP HANA, Apache Spark)
U	HIGH MEMORY	High memory and bare metal performance – use for in memory DBs including SAP HANA
Z	HGH COMPUTE & MEMORY	Fast CPU, high memory and NVMe–based SSDs – use when high overall performance is required
H	HIGH DISK THROUGHPUT	Up to 16 TB of HDD–based local storage

When deploying an instance on AWS, the first step is to select an Amazon Machine Image (AMI). An AMI is essentially a template that includes the information required to launch an instance in EC2. An AMI includes the following:

- A template for the root volume for the instance (for example, an operating system, an application server and applications)

- Launch permissions that control which AWS accounts can use the AMI to launch instances

- A block device mapping that specifies the storage volumes to attach to the instance when it's launched

AWS provide a number of AMIs based on various operating systems and configurations. You can also select from the AWS Marketplace, AMIs that have been shared by the community, and your own AMIs that you have previously saved (registered).

AMAZON EBS & SNAPSHOTS

Most EC2 instance types use the Elastic Block Store (EBS) for persistent storage. EBS volumes are durable, block-level storage volumes that can be attached to a single EC2 instance. There are a several different volume types available that differ in performance characteristics and price. These include:

- General Purpose SSD (gp2)
- Provisioned IOPS SSD (io1)
- Throughput Optimized HDD (st1)
- Cold HDD (sc1)
- Magnetic (standard, a previous-generation type)

Each EBS volume is replicated across multiple systems within an Availability Zone (described below) to avoid the risk of data loss if a single hardware component fails. Additionally, users can take snapshots of their EBS volumes which are a point-in-time copy of the data.

Snapshots are incremental backups, which means that only the blocks on the device that have changed after your most recent snapshot are saved.

AWS INFRASTRUCTURE SERVICES

There are a number of supporting services and features on AWS that enable compute instances to be launched in a functional state. These include:

- **Virtual Private Cloud (VPC)** – A VPC is a virtual network that provides the networking layer of EC2. A VPC can be configured to your own requirements
- **Elastic Block Store (EBS)** – EBS provides persistent block-based storage volumes that can be attached to EC2 instances

Amazon VPCs are created within AWS Regions, which is a separate geographic area in which multiple Availability Zones (AZs, which are essentially data centers) are located. Amazon provide more information on regions and availability zones here:

https://docs.aws.amazon.com/AWSEC2/latest/UserGuide/using-regions-availability-zones.html.

Subnets are created within AZs and this is where Amazon EC2 instances are deployed. The following diagram depicts this AWS infrastructure:

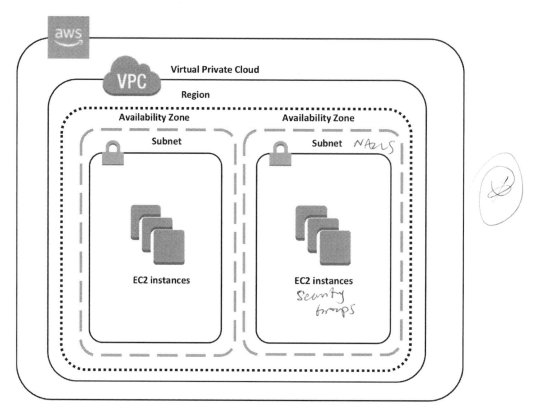

Additionally, to be able to connect to your EC2 instances on the AWS cloud, it is necessary to configure Security Groups - which are firewalls at the instance level - and Network Access Control Lists (NACLs) - which are firewalls at the subnet level.

When a VPC has been properly configured (EC2 instances have been launched with public IP addresses, and Security Groups and NACLs have been configured with the correct rules) it is then possible to directly access EC2 instances from the Internet.

The following simplified diagram depicts the configuration elements required to connect to an Amazon EC2 instance from the Internet.

The diagram shows two EC2 instances with separate security groups but in the same subnet within a VPC. An Internet Gateway provides the Internet connectivity - and in this configuration each EC2 instance would require a public IP address:

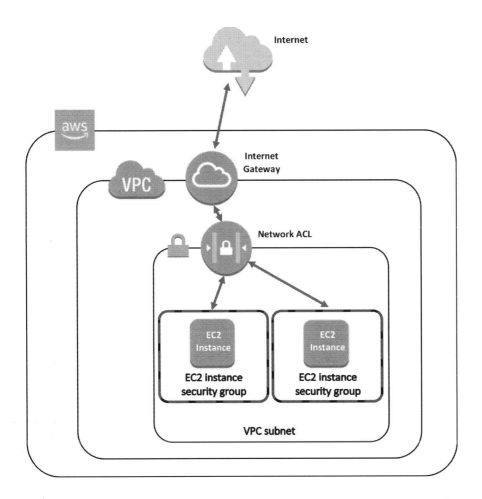

Logging on to EC2 instances involves usage of a key pair (cryptographic key) that you generate through the console and in some cases a password.

LOAD BALANCING AND AUTO SCALING

Cloud applications are usually deployed in an architecture where multiple instances can share the incoming traffic load and individual instances can be easily added or removed as the load varies up or down.

AWS provide a couple of services that assist with distributing incoming connections and automatically ensuring the right number of instances are available to service the load. These are Elastic Load Balancing and EC2 Auto Scaling.

The following diagram depicts an Elastic Load Balancer (ELB) servicing a number of EC2 instances across two Availability Zones. Connections from multiple devices hit the ELB which then distributes the connections evenly across the EC2 instances.

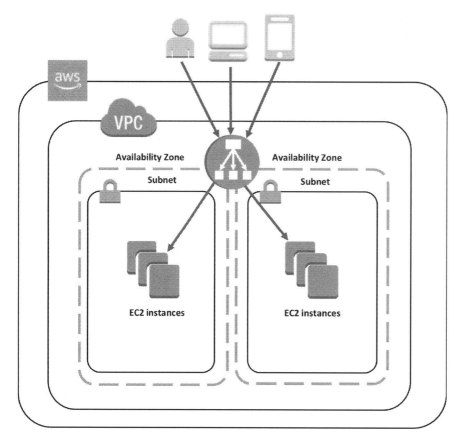

Elastic Load Balancing provides the following benefits:

- High availability – ELB automatically distributes traffic across multiple EC2 instances in different AZs within a region

- Security – ELB provides robust security features, including integrated certificate management, user-authentication and SSL/TLS decryption

- Elasticity – ELB is capable of handling rapid changes in network traffic patterns

EC2 Auto Scaling can complement the architecture depicted in the diagram above by dynamically scaling the number of EC2 instances based on current demand.

EC2 Auto Scaling provides the following benefits:

- Fault tolerance – Auto Scaling detects when an instance is unhealthy and replaces it

- Scalability and elasticity – Auto Scaling automatically scales the number of instances servicing your application based on demand

STORAGE

INTRODUCTION TO STORAGE

In cloud computing, cloud storage is a service offering with which a consumer is able to read and write data to cloud-based systems that are managed by a service provider. We will discuss the basic concepts you need to understand to get started with storage on AWS.

Cloud storage is usually accessible through a web service or application programming interface (API). The underlying infrastructure is typically a virtualized infrastructure stack with disk drives that are managed by a software service layer.

The most common form of cloud storage is object storage but any method of data management that can be offered as a service across a network can be used. The other cloud storage options are block-based storage and file-based storage. All of these will be discussed within this section.

STORAGE CONCEPTS

Hard Disk Drives (HDD) have been around for a long while and are still in widespread use today. An HDD is a mechanical drive with spinning platters and a head that floats above the platters and moves into position to read and write data.

HDDs are also known as magnetic drives as they use magnetic polarization to record a one or zero value.

The performance of an HDD depends on a number of factors and these include the following measurements:

- **Revolutions Per Minute (RPM)** – the speed of rotation of the platters
- **Seek time** – the mean time it takes to move the head of a disk drive from one track to another
- **Input / Output Operations Per Second (IOPS)** – the number of IO transactions per second
- **Throughput** – the data transfer rate of a drive

HDDs provide good throughput, large capacity, and are extremely low cost.

Solid State Drives (SSD) store data on non-volatile microchips and have no moving parts. Non-volatile SSD chips differ from computer memory in that the data is retained when power is removed.

SSDs offer extremely high IOPS performance when compared to HDDs and also provide good throughput. SSDs are also much more expensive.

MEASURING DATA

Stored data is typically measured using the decimal system in kilobytes (kB), Megabytes (MB), Gigabytes (GB), Terabytes (TB) and Petabytes (PB).

In some cases, the binary prefix is used such as gibibyte (GiB). A gibibyte is equal to 1024 mebibytes (MiB) while a gigabyte (GB) is equal to 1000 megabytes (MB).

To confuse matters, a GB of computer memory is equal to 1024 MB (rather than 1000 MB) and some storage manufacturers have been known to use this measurement for disks too.

The following table shows how each term relates to the other in both the decimal and binary formats and the values are the number of bytes (a byte is 8 bits).

Decimal Name	Decimal Abbr.	Decimal Value	Binary Name	Binary Abbr.	Binary Value
Kilobyte	kB	1,000	Kibibyte	kiB	1,024
Megabyte	MB	1,000,000	Mebibyte	MiB	1,048,576
Gigabyte	GB	1,000,000,000	Gibibyte	GiB	1,073,741,824
Terabyte	TB	1,000,000,000,000	Tebibyte	TiB	1,099,511,627,776

The following link provides some more background on this subject:

https://en.wikipedia.org/wiki/Gibibyte

DATA ACCESSIBILITY SLAS

Cloud service providers will often provide service level agreements (SLAs) for the availability and durability of their storage systems.

Availability relates to system uptime, i.e. the amount of time per month or year that the storage system is operational and can deliver data upon request. Service providers aim to increase availability by designing highly available and fault tolerant storage systems.

Availability is usually expressed as a percentage of uptime in a given year. The following table shows some common availability SLAs and how much downtime each corresponds with:

Availability %	Downtime Per Month	Downtime Per Year
99% ("two nines")	7.3 hours	3.65 days
99.5% ("two and a half nines")	3.65 hours	1.83 days
99.9% ("three nines")	44 mins	8.77 hours
99.95% ("three and a half nines")	22 mins	4.38 hours
99.99% ("four nines")	4.38 mins	52 mins

Durability relates to measuring the amount of data that may be lost due to errors occurring when writing data. In other words, durability measures the likelihood of losing some of your data.

Durability is usually expressed as a percentage of reliability and can also be interpreted as the number of files that are likely to be lost in a given year.

The following table shows the four Amazon Simple Storage Service (S3) storage classes with their respective durability SLAs and how many files could be lost per year:

AWS Storage Class	Durability %	Files lost per year per PB
Amazon S3 RRS	99.99% ("four nines")	12 million
S3 Standard	99.999999999% ("eleven nines")	.12 (one every 8 years)
S3 Standard – IA	99.999999999% ("eleven nines")	.12 (one every 8 years)
Standard	99.999999999% ("eleven nines")	.12 (one every 8 years)

CLOUD STORAGE TYPES

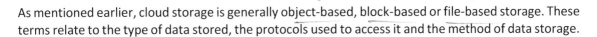

As mentioned earlier, cloud storage is generally object-based, block-based or file-based storage. These terms relate to the type of data stored, the protocols used to access it and the method of data storage.

Object Storage

With object storage, data is managed as individual objects rather than a file hierarchy (as with a traditional file system). Each object includes the data itself, metadata (data about the data), and a globally unique identifier.

Due to its flat file structure, object storage has virtually unlimited scalability and allows the retention of massive amounts of unstructured data. The data is often replicated across multiple physical systems and facilities providing high availability and durability.

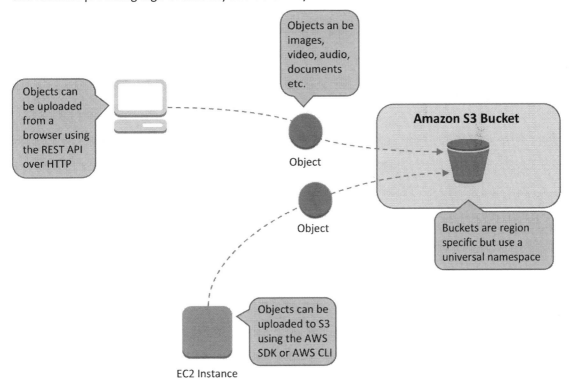

Object storage is usually accessed over Representational State Transfer (REST) and Simple Object Access Protocol (SOAP) over Hypertext Transfer Protocol (HTTP).

The Amazon Simple Storage Service (S3) is a key, value object-based storage system built to store and retrieve huge amounts of data from any source.

Objects in S3 are stored in a flat structure with no hierarchy. The top level containers within which objects are stored are known as buckets. Though there is no hierarchy, S3 does support the concept of folders for organization (grouping of objects).

There are several S3 storage classes with varying levels of availability, durability and features. The standard class offers the following features:

- Low latency and high throughput performance
- Designed for durability of 99.999999999% of objects across multiple Availability Zones
- Data is resilient in the event of one entire Availability Zone destruction
- Designed for 99.99% availability over a given year
- Backed with the Amazon S3 Service Level Agreement for availability
- Supports SSL for data in transit and encryption of data at rest
- Lifecycle management for automatic migration of objects

Common use cases for object storage include backup, application hosting, media hosting and software delivery.

Block Storage — EBS

Data is stored and managed in blocks within sectors and tracks and is controlled by a server-based operating system. Block storage volumes appear as local disks to the operating system and can be partitioned and formatted.

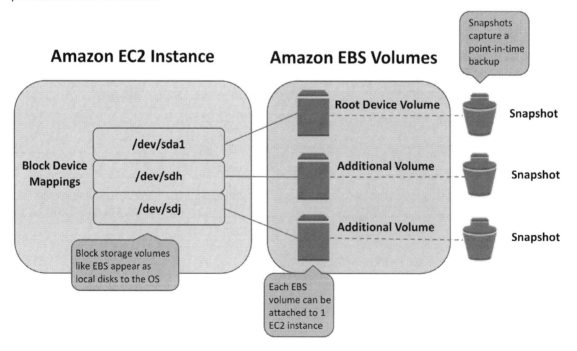

Block storage is typically used in Storage Area Network (SAN) environments that use the Fibre Channel (FC) protocol as well as Ethernet networks using protocols such as iSCSI or Fibre Channel over Ethernet (FCoE).

Block storage is typically more expensive than object or file storage but provides low latency, and high and consistent performance. The costs are often highest in SAN implementations due to the specialized equipment required.

Amazon Elastic Block Store (EBS) is the AWS service for block storage. EBS provides persistent block storage volumes for use with EC2 instances in the AWS cloud.

There are several EBS volume types to choose from with varying characteristics as can be seen in the table below:

	Solid State Drives (SSD)		Hard Disk Drives (HDD)	
Volume Type	General Purpose SSD (gp2)	Provisioned IOPS SSD (io1)	Throughput Optimized (st1)	Cold HDD (sc1)
Description	Balance of price to performance	High performance SSD	Low cost HDD	Lowest cost HDD
Use Cases	• Most workloads • System boot volumes • Virtual desktops	• Critical business apps that require sustained IOPS performance • Apps that require more than 10,000 IOPS or 160 MiB/s • Large database workloads	• Streaming workloads with fast throughput • Low price • Big data • Data warehouses	• Throughput oriented storage for large volumes of infrequently accessed data • Lowest cost • Cannot be a boot volume
Volume Size	1 GiB – 16 TiB	4 GiB – 16 TiB	500 GiB – 16 TiB	500 GiB – 16 TiB
Max IOPS Per Volume	10,000	32,000	500	250
Max Throughput Per Volume	160 MiB/s	500 MiB/s	500 MiB/s	250 MiB/s

Common use cases for block storage are structured information such as file systems, databases, transactional logs, SQL databases and virtual machines (VMs).

Though the cloud service provider takes care of many aspects of performance and availability, it is also possible to implement a Redundant Array of Inexpensive Disks (RAID) array on Amazon EBS.

File Storage

File storage servers store data in a hierarchical structure using files and folders. Data is accessed as file IDs across a network using either the Server Message Block (SMB) for Windows, or Network File System (NFS) for Unix/Linux.

A file system is mounted via the network to a client computer where it then becomes accessible for reading and writing data. Files and folders can be created, updated, and deleted.

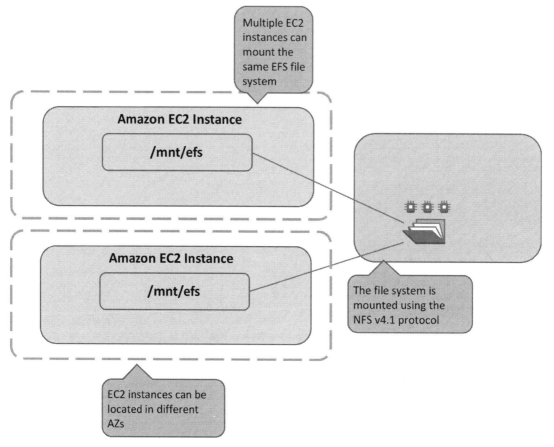

Only file-level operations can occur on a mounted file system. It is not possible to issue block level commands or format or partition the underlying storage volumes.

File storage is easy to implement and use and is generally quite inexpensive. Use cases include web serving and content management, shared corporate directories, home drives, database backups and big data analytics workloads.

The Amazon Elastic File System (EFS) is a simple, scalable, elastic file storage in the AWS cloud that is based on NFS. EFS provides the ability to mount a file system to many EC2 instances simultaneously and can achieve high levels of aggregate throughput and IOPS.

EFS is a regional AWS service and provides high availability and durability by storing data redundantly across Availability Zones (AZs).

NETWORK

INTRODUCTION TO NETWORK

In modern networking, network functions are increasingly becoming abstracted from the underlying switching and routing hardware layer. These virtualized resources are usually API driven, allowing developers to create, update and delete software-based network interfaces, firewalls, load balancers and routing functions through code.

Public cloud providers such as AWS offer many network services to customers that can be configured through graphical interfaces, command line and API endpoints. We will discuss the basic concepts you need to understand to get started with network services on AWS.

There are a few supporting concepts that are important to understand if you're working with networking in the cloud that I'll cover off first. These include IP subnetting, routing and gateways, the OSI model and network virtualization.

IP ADDRESSING

Whatever your role in IT, you'll likely need to understand IP addressing to some level. In the cloud you need to understand how to define the IP subnet address ranges your cloud resources will use and the difference between private and public addresses (at a minimum).

An Internet Protocol (IP) address is a label used to identify a computer on a shared network. There are two versions of IP in common use today: version 4 and version 6.

IPv4 has been around for much longer and is the most well used address range but IPv6, which has a much larger address space, is becoming increasingly common, and is supported by many **AWS services** today.

As IPv4 is the default protocol used on AWS, I'll exclude IPv6 from the rest of the discussion. However, it is worth understanding IPv6 and how and why it is used. You can get more information on IPv6 on Wikipedia.

An IPv4 address is a 32-bit number which provides up to 4,294,967,296 possible addresses. Each address consists of a network identifier (which represents the network or subnet) and a host identifier (which represents the individual network attached device).

A subnet mask is a prefix that determines which portions of the address represent the network and which represent the hosts (devices). The following diagram depicts this:

Network   Host

IP Address: 192.168.100.10
Subnet Mask: 255.255.255.0

With a /24 subnet mask 8 bits are left for hosts (up to 255 host addresses)

The subnet mask indicates the network portion of the address. This is a 24 bit mask (/24)

A classful network design was created back in the 80s that used three classes of network (A, B & C) based on the first octet of the address and using strict octet boundaries for the entire address. This proved to lack the scalability required for the expansion of the Internet and so a classless network design was created. This is known as Classless Inter-Domain Routing (CIDR).

With CIDR variable length subnet masks can be used to allow more granular and efficient use of addresses. An example of CIDR usage is the private address space, which is a reserved address space meant for computers not directly connected to the Internet.

The table below shows how a more granular approach can be taken to allocating addresses:

CIDR Block	Subnet Mask	Max Subnets	Hosts Per Subnet
192.168.0.0/26	255.255.255.192	1024	62
192.168.0.0/27	255.255.255.224	2048	30
192.168.0.0/28	255.255.255.240	4096	14

The CIDR blocks in the table above would allow the creation of subnets with just the right numbers of hosts. This is an efficient way of assigning address blocks.

ROUTING AND GATEWAYS

IP addresses are the means of identifying a unique device on a network. To get to a device across a network, a method of determining the best path to get there is required.

This is where routers come in. A router uses a routing protocol (or it may be directly configured) to learn the best path to reach a destination network. This data is held in a routing table.

A router is also considered a gateway when devices on a network are pointed towards it by way of a default gateway address. This address is configured in the IP settings of the networked device and specifies the target for all traffic that is destined to networks other than the local network.

THE OSI MODEL

The Open Systems Interconnection model (OSI model) is a conceptual model that characterizes and standardizes the communication functions of communication and computing systems.

The OSI model divides data communication into 7 abstraction layers and standardizes protocols into groups of networking functionality that ensure interoperability between diverse systems irrespective of the underlying technology.

It's important to understand the 7 layers of the OSI model and where common protocols are located.

The following diagram depicts the 7 layers of the OSI model:

OSI Layer	Data Unit	Function / Protocols
7. Application	Data	Network process to application HTTP, SMTP, IMAP, SNMP, POP3, FTP
6. Presentation		Data representation and encryption ASCII, JPEG, MPEG, SSL, TLS, compression
5. Session		Inter-host communication NetBIOS, RPC, NFS
4. Transport	Segments	End-to-end communications and reliability TCP, UDP
3. Network	Packet/Datagram	Path determination & logical addressing (IP) IPv4, IPv6, ICMP, IPSec, ARP
2. Data Link	Bit/Frame	Physical addressing (MAC & LLC) Ethernet, 802.1x, PPP, ATM, Fiber Channel, MAC, MPLS, PPP
1. Physical	Bit	Media, signal and binary transmission Cables, connectors, hubs

A brief description of the seven layers of the OSI model can be found on Webopedia.

NETWORK VIRTUALIZATION

Two commonly used terms related to network virtualization are Software Defined Networking (SDN) and Network Functions Virtualization (NFV).

SDN refers to the ability to control the behavior of network devices programmatically. Usually SDN implementations offer centralized control, separation of control and forwarding functions, and the ability to programmatically control behavior using well-defined interfaces.

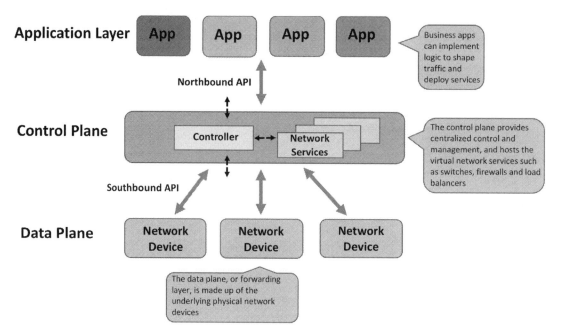

NFV is an approach whereby standard compute virtualization technologies are used to host network services that would traditionally run on dedicated proprietary hardware. With NFV, Virtual Machines (VMs) can run network functions such as routing, load balancing and firewalls.

SDN and NFV are considered to be complementary technologies that can be implemented together resulting in virtualized network functions that can be centrally controlled through software.

VIRTUAL PRIVATE CLOUD (VPC)

An Amazon Virtual Private Cloud (VPC) is an isolated network environment on AWS that is analogous to having a private data center in the cloud.

With a VPC, you can specify your own CIDR address block, create subnets and configure route tables and gateways. VPC allows the creation of both IPv4 and IPv6 addresses. VPCs are created within AWS regions.

Subnets

A VPC subnet is created within an Availability zone (AZ) which is comprised of one or more data centers within an AWS region. There are two or more AZs in each region and you can create many subnets in each AZ.

Each subnet can be configured as either private or public. With a private subnet, instances are only assigned a private IP address (not routable on the Internet) and can only communicate with the outside world by way of a network address translation (NAT) device such as an AWS NAT Gateway.

A public subnet is a subnet in which instances are assigned a public IP address (in addition to a private IP address) and to which an Internet Gateway (IGW) is connected. This is essentially the default gateway for the instances in the subnet.

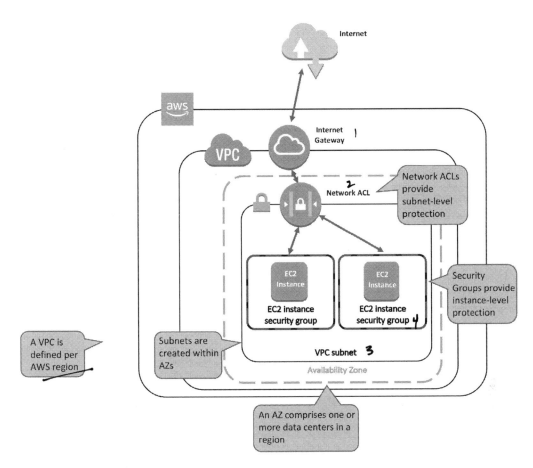

Route Tables

A route table contains a set of rules, called routes, that are used to determine where network traffic is directed. Each subnet in a VPC must be associated to a route table. A subnet can only be assigned to one route table, but a route table can be assigned to multiple subnets.

An "implicit" router is associated with all VPCs and ensures that routing works between all the subnets you create. Each route in a route table specifies a destination CIDR and a target, and the router will use the most specific route that matches the traffic when making forwarding decisions.

Load Balancing

Load balancing is a method of efficiently distributing incoming network traffic across a series of backend servers or targets. With a load balancer you can evenly distribute connections to multiple servers ensuring high availability and reliability as well as providing scalability as the number of requests increases or decreases.

The AWS Elastic Load Balancing service is provided within the Elastic Compute Cloud (EC2) console and there are three different types of ELB available for use with your EC2 instances. These are:

- **Application Load Balancer (ALB)** – layer 7 load balancer that routes connections based on the content of the request

- **Network Load Balancer (NLB)** – layer 4 load balancer that routes connections based on IP protocol data

- **Classic Load Balancer (CLB)** – this is the oldest of the three and provides basic load balancing at both layer 4 and layer 7

VPN and Direct Connect

A virtual private network (VPN) is used to extend a private network across a public or untrusted network. On AWS you can create an IPsec VPN connection between your VPC and your remote network, which could be your company's on-premise data center.

Another option is AWS Direct Connect which is a network service that provides an alternative to using the Internet to connect a customer's on-premise sites to AWS. With AWS Direct Connect, data is transmitted through a private network connection between AWS and a customer's datacenter or corporate network.

Security

There are a number of tools and services to secure your resources in your VPC. A Security Group is an instance-level virtual firewall that controls inbound and outbound traffic. A Network ACL is a subnet-level firewall controlling traffic in and out of your subnets.

Security Group	Network ACL
Operates at the instance (interface) level	Operates at the subnet level
Supports allow rules only	Supports allow and deny rules
Stateful	Stateless
Evaluates all rules	Processes rules in order
Applies to an instance only if associated with a group	Automatically applies to all instances in the subnets its associated with

The AWS Web Application Firewall (WAF) protects web applications from common web exploits that could affect application availability, compromise security or consume excessive resources. AWS WAF provides control over which traffic to allow or block to web applications through the definition of customizable web security rules.

AWS Shield is a managed Distributed Denial of Service (DDoS) protection service that safeguards applications running on AWS. AWS Shield offers always-on protection and provides detection and mitigation against sophisticated DDoS attacks at the network, transport and application layers.

CLOUD COMPUTING CONCEPTS

The remainder of the book from this section onwards is the actual training notes that relate directly to the knowledge you need for the AWS Certified Cloud Practitioner exam.

Please note that the content is mostly delivered in a succinct, bullet-point format to help you get straight to the key facts you need to know for the exam.

GENERAL CLOUD COMPUTING CONCEPTS

Cloud computing is the on-demand delivery of compute power, database storage, applications and other IT resources through a cloud services platform via the Internet with pay-as-you-go pricing.

Cloud computing provides a simple way to access servers, storage, databases and a broad set of application services over the Internet.

A cloud services platform such as Amazon Web Services owns and maintains the network-connected hardware required for these application services, while you provision and use what you need via a web application.

THE SIX ADVANTAGES

AWS promote the six advantages of cloud:

1. Trade capital expense for variable expense
2. Benefit from massive economies of scale
3. Stop guessing about capacity
4. Increase speed and agility
5. Stop spending money running and maintaining data centers
6. Go global in minutes

TRADE CAPITAL EXPENSE FOR VARIABLE EXPENSE

Instead of having to invest heavily in data centers and servers before you know how you're going to use them, you can pay only when you consume computing resources, and pay only for how much you consume.

BENEFIT FROM MASSIVE ECONOMIES OF SCALE

By using cloud computing, you can achieve a lower variable cost than you can get on your own. As usage from hundreds of thousands of customers is aggregated in the cloud, providers such as AWS can achieve higher economies of scale, which translates into lower pay as-you-go prices.

STOP GUESSING ABOUT CAPACITY

When you make a capacity decision prior to deploying an application, you often end up either sitting on expensive idle resources or dealing with limited capacity. With cloud computing, you eliminate guessing on your infrastructure capacity needs. You can access as much or as little capacity as you need and scale up and down as required with only a few minutes notice.

INCREASE SPEED AND AGILITY

In a cloud computing environment, new IT resources are only a click away, which means that you reduce the time to make those resources available to your developers from weeks to just minutes. This results in a dramatic increase in agility for the organization, since the cost and time it takes to experiment and develop is significantly lower

STOP SPENDING MONEY RUNNING AND MAINTAINING DATA CENTERS

Focus on projects that differentiate your business, not the infrastructure. Cloud computing lets you focus on your own customers, rather than on the heavy lifting of racking, stacking, and powering servers.

GO GLOBAL IN MINUTES

Easily deploy your application in multiple regions around the world with just a few clicks. This means you can provide lower latency and a better experience for your customers at minimal cost.

TYPES OF CLOUD COMPUTING

3 types of cloud computing model:

- Infrastructure as a service (IaaS)
- Platform as a service (PaaS)
- Software as a service (SaaS)

Infrastructure as a Service (IaaS)

Infrastructure as a Service (IaaS) contains the basic building blocks for cloud IT and typically provide access to networking features, computers (virtual or on dedicated hardware) and data storage space.

IaaS provides you with the highest level of flexibility and management control over your IT resources and is most similar to existing IT resources that many IT departments and developers are familiar with today.

Platform as a Service (PaaS)

Platform as a Service (PaaS) removes the need for your organization to manage the underlying infrastructure (usually hardware and operating systems) and allows you to focus on the deployment and management of your applications.

This helps you be more efficient as you don't need to worry about resource procurement, capacity planning, software maintenance, patching, or any of the other undifferentiated heavy lifting involved in running your application.

Software as a Service (SaaS)

Software as a Service (SaaS) provides you with a completed product that is run and managed by the service provider. In most cases, people referring to Software as a Service are referring to end-user applications.

With a SaaS offering you do not have to think about how the service is maintained or how the underlying infrastructure is managed; you only need to think about how you will use that particular piece of software.

A common example of a SaaS application is web-based email which you can use to send and receive email without having to manage feature additions to the email product or maintain the servers and operating systems that the email program is running on.

This provides high availability, fault tolerance, scalability and elasticity.

TYPES OF CLOUD DEPLOYMENT

There are 3 types of cloud deployment:

1. Public Cloud or simple "Cloud" – e.g. AWS, Azure, GCP

2. Hybrid Cloud – mixture of public and private clouds

3. Private Cloud (on-premise) – managed in your own data center, e.g. Hyper-V, OpenStack, VMware

Public Cloud

A cloud-based application is fully deployed in the cloud and all parts of the application run in the cloud. Applications in the cloud have either been created in the cloud or have been migrated from an existing infrastructure to take advantage of the benefits of cloud computing.

Cloud-based applications can be built on low-level infrastructure pieces or can use higher level services that provide abstraction from the management, architecting, and scaling requirements of core infrastructure.

Hybrid

A hybrid deployment is a way to connect infrastructure and applications between cloud-based resources and existing resources that are not located in the cloud.

The most common method of hybrid deployment is between the cloud and existing on-premises infrastructure to extend and grow an organization's infrastructure into the cloud while connecting cloud resources to the internal system.

On-premises

The deployment of resources on-premises using virtualization and resource management tools, is sometimes called the "private cloud."

On-premises deployment doesn't provide many of the benefits of cloud computing but is sometimes sought for its ability to provide dedicated resources.

In most cases, this deployment model is the same as legacy IT infrastructure while using application management and virtualization technologies to try and increase resource utilization.

AWS GLOBAL INFRASTRUCTURE

GENERAL

AWS Global Infrastructure is a key technology area covered in the Cloud Practitioner exam blueprint. The AWS infrastructure is built around Regions and Availability Zones (AZs).

An AWS Region is a physical location in the world where AWS have multiple AZs.

AZs consist of one or more discrete data centers, each with redundant power, networking, and connectivity, housed in separate facilities.

Each region is completely independent. Each Availability Zone is isolated, but the Availability Zones in a region are connected through low-latency links.

AWS are constantly expanding around the world and currently there are:

- 21 regions
- 66 availability zones

The following diagram shows the AWS global infrastructure with regions (orange circles, green are new regions), and availability zones (the number of AZs is specified within each region):

REGIONS

A region is a geographical area.

Each region consists of 2 or more availability zones.

Each Amazon Region is designed to be completely isolated from the other Amazon Regions.

Each AWS Region has multiple Availability Zones and data centers.

You can replicate data within a region and between regions using private or public Internet connections.

You retain complete control and ownership over the region in which your data is physically located, making it easy to meet regional compliance and data residency requirements.

Note that there is a charge for data transfer between regions.

When you launch an EC2 instance, you must select an AMI that's in the same region. If the AMI is in another region, you can copy the AMI to the region you're using.

Regions and Endpoints:

- When you work with an instance using the command line interface or API actions, you must specify its regional endpoint.

- To reduce data latency in your applications, most Amazon Web Services offer a regional endpoint to make your requests.

- An endpoint is a URL that is the entry point for a web service.

- For example, https://dynamodb.us-west-2.amazonaws.com is an entry point for the Amazon DynamoDB service.

AVAILABILITY ZONES

Availability Zones are physically separate and isolated from each other.

AZs span one or more data centers and have direct, low-latency, high throughput and redundant network connections between each other.

Each AZ is designed as an independent failure zone.

When you launch an instance, you can select an Availability Zone or let AWS choose one for you.

If you distribute your EC2 instances across multiple Availability Zones and one instance fails, you can design your application so that an instance in another Availability Zone can handle requests.

You can also use Elastic IP addresses to mask the failure of an instance in one Availability Zone by rapidly remapping the address to an instance in another Availability Zone.

An Availability Zone is represented by a region code followed by a letter identifier; for example, **us-east-1a.**

To ensure that resources are distributed across the Availability Zones for a region, AWS independently map Availability Zones to names for each AWS account.

For example, the Availability Zone **us-east-1a** for your AWS account might not be the same location as us-east-1a for another AWS account.

To coordinate Availability Zones across accounts, you must use the *AZ ID*, which is a unique and consistent identifier for an Availability Zone.

AZs are physically separated within a typical metropolitan region and are located in lower risk flood plains.

AZs use discrete UPS and onsite backup generation facilities and are fed via different grids from independent facilities.

AZs are all redundantly connected to multiple tier-1 transit providers.

The following diagram depicts a region with 2 availability zones:

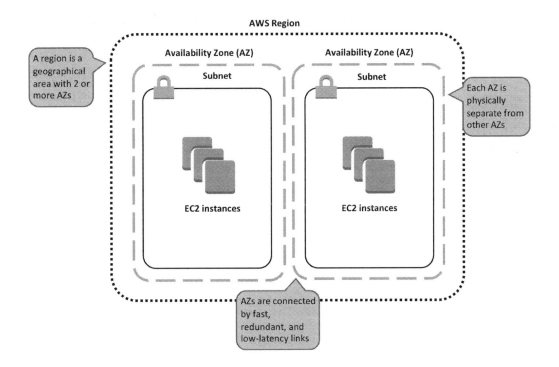

EDGE LOCATIONS AND REGIONAL EDGE CACHES

Edge locations are Content Delivery Network (CDN) endpoints for CloudFront.

There are many more edge locations than regions.   ↳ Content Delivery Network

Currently there are over 100 edge locations.

Regional Edge Caches sit between your CloudFront Origin servers and the Edge Locations.

A Regional Edge Cache has a larger cache-width than each of the individual Edge Locations.

The following diagram shows CloudFront Edge locations and Regional Edge Caches:

AWS GLOBAL INFRASTRUCTURE QUIZ QUESTIONS

Answers and explanations are provided below after the last question in this section.

Question 1: What is an availability zone composed of?

A. A collection of edge locations

B. A collection of VPCs

C. One or more DCs in a location

D. One or more regions

Question 2: Which service of the following services is global in scope?

A. AWS Identity and Access Management (IAM)

B. Amazon Elastic Compute Cloud (EC2)

C. Amazon Relational Database Service (RDS)

D. AWS Lambda

Question 3: What are the three fundamentals of pricing in AWS?

A. Compute, storage and inbound data transfer

B. Compute, database and Internet connectivity

C. Compute, storage and outbound data transfer

D. Elasticity, agility, and data transfer

Question 4: Which pricing model is highly flexible with no long-term commitments or upfront payments?

A. Dedicated instances

B. Spot instances

C. On-demand

D. Reservations

Question 5: What is an AWS Region composed of?

A. Two or more Virtual Private Clouds (VPC)

B. Two or more availability zones

C. At least one availability zone

D. A collection of EC2 instances

© 2021 Digital Cloud Training
AWS Certified Cloud Practitioner - Training Notes

| 46

Question 6: Which AWS policy defines the prohibited uses of the AWS Cloud?

A. AWS End User Policy

B. AWS Cloud Policy

C. AWS Acceptable Practices Policy

D. AWS Acceptable Use Policy

Choosing the right region:
- Data Sovereignty Laws
- Latency to End users
- AWS Services

(D)

AWS GLOBAL INFRASTRUCTURE ANSWERS

Question 1, Answer: C

Explanation:

A is incorrect. An availability zone is not a collection of edge locations.

B is incorrect. An availability zone is not a collection of VPCs.

C is correct. Availability Zones are physically separate and isolated from each other. They are located in one or more data centers in a geographical area.

D is incorrect. Availability zones are contained within regions, not the other way around.

Question 2, Answer: A

Explanation:

A is correct. The AWS IAM service is a global service which means you create your users, groups, roles and policies in one place.

B is incorrect. The Amazon EC2 service is a regional service which means you launch compute resources into a region.

C is incorrect. The Amazon RDS service is a regional service which means you launch database resources into a region.

D is incorrect. The AWS Lambda service is a regional service which means you launch compute "functions" into a region.

Question 3, Answer: C

Explanation:

A is incorrect. You don't pay for inbound data transfer.

B is incorrect. Internet connectivity is not a fundamental of AWS pricing.

C is correct. Compute, storage and outbound data transfer are the three fundamentals of AWS pricing.

D is incorrect. These are not fundamentals of AWS pricing. Data transfer is charged but only outbound.

Question 4, Answer: C

Explanation:

A is incorrect. Dedicated instances are used when you need to run workloads on hardware that's dedicated to a single customer.

B is incorrect. Spot instances are where you purchase spare capacity with no commitments. However, it is less flexible than on-demand as you can't control when capacity will be available

C is correct. On-demand is the best option when you need the most flexibility. There are no long-term commitments or upfront payments.

D is incorrect as Reservations are used to get up to 75% discount from the on-demand rate in exchange for a term commitment.

Question 5, Answer: B

Explanation:

A is incorrect. Virtual Private Clouds (VPCs), which will be discussed later in the course, are contained within a region but it's not necessary to have more than one VPC in a region.

B is correct. Every region has at least 2 availability zones which are composed of one or more data centers

C is incorrect. There are always at least 2 availability zones in a region

D is incorrect. EC2 instances, which are computer instances, run in a VPC and within a region, but this is not how we define a region.

Question 6, Answer: D

Explanation:

A is incorrect. There is no policy called the "AWS End User Policy".

B is incorrect. There is no policy called the "AWS Cloud Policy".

C is incorrect. This is incorrect, there is no policy called the "AWS Acceptable Practices Policy".

D is correct. The AWS Acceptable Use Policy describes the prohibited uses of AWS.

IDENTITY AND ACCESS MANAGEMENT

GENERAL IAM CONCEPTS

AWS Identity and Access Management (IAM) is a web service that helps you securely control access to AWS resources.

You use IAM to control who is authenticated (signed in) and authorized (has permissions) to use resources.

IAM makes it easy to provide multiple users secure access to AWS resources.

When you first create an AWS account, you begin with a single sign-in identity that has complete access to all AWS services and resources in the account.

This identity is called the AWS account root user and is accessed by signing in with the email address and password that you used to create the account.

IAM can be used to manage:

- Users
- Groups
- Access policies
- Roles
- User credentials
- User password policies
- Multi-factor authentication (MFA)
- API keys for programmatic access (CLI)

Provides centralized control of your AWS account.

Enables shared access to your AWS account.

IAM provides the following features:

- Shared access to your AWS account
- Granular permissions
- Secure access to AWS resources for application that run on Amazon EC2
- Multi-Factor authentication
- Identity federation
- Identity information for assurance
- PCI DSS compliance
- Integrated with may AWS services
- Eventually consistent
- Free to use

You can work with AWS Identity and Access Management in any of the following ways:

- AWS Management Console
- AWS Command Line Tools  Exam
- AWS SDK
- IAM HTTPS API

By default, new users are created with NO access to any AWS services – they can only login to the AWS console.

Permission must be explicitly granted to allow a user to access an AWS service.

IAM users are individuals who have been granted access to an AWS account.

Each IAM user has three main components:

- A username
- A password
- Permissions to access various resources

You can apply granular permissions with IAM.

You can assign users individual security credentials such as access keys, passwords, and multi-factor authentication devices.

IAM is not used for application-level authentication.

Identity Federation (including AD, Facebook etc.) can be configured allowing secure access to resources in an AWS account without creating an IAM user account.

Multi-factor authentication (MFA) can be enabled/enforced for the AWS account and for individual users under the account.

MFA uses an authentication device that continually generates random, six-digit, single-use authentication codes.

You can authenticate using an MFA device in the following two ways:

- Through the AWS Management Console – the user is prompted for a username, password and authentication code.
- Using the AWS API – restrictions are added to IAM policies and developers can request temporary security credentials and pass MFA parameters in their AWS STS API requests.
- Using the AWS CLI by obtaining temporary security credentials from STS (aws sts get-session-token).

It is a best practice to always setup multi-factor authentication on the root account.

IAM is universal (global) and does not apply to regions. Exam

IAM is eventually consistent.

IAM replicates data across multiple data centers around the world.

The "root account" is the account created when you setup the AWS account. It has complete Admin access and is the only account that has this access by default. Exam

It is a best practice to not use the root account for anything other than billing.

Power user access allows all permissions except the management of groups and users in IAM.

Temporary security credentials consist of the AWS access key ID, secret access key and security token.

IAM can assign temporary security credentials to provide users with temporary access to services/resources.

To sign-in you must provide your account ID or account alias in addition to a username and password.

The sign-in URL includes the account ID or account alias, e.g.:

https://My_AWS_Account_ID.signin.aws.amazon.com/console/

Alternatively, you can sign-in at the following URL and enter your account ID or alias manually:

https://console.aws.amazon.com/

IAM integrates with many different AWS services.

IAM supports PCI DSS compliance.

AWS recommend that you use the AWS SDKs to make programmatic API calls to IAM.

However, you can also use the IAM Query API to make direct calls to the IAM web service.

AUTHENTICATION METHODS

Console password:

- A password that the user can enter to sign-in to interactive sessions such as the AWS Management Console.

- You can allow users to change their own passwords.

- You can allow selected IAM users to change their passwords by disabling the option for all users and using an IAM policy to grant permissions for the selected users.

Access Keys:

- A combination of an **access key ID** and a **secret access key.**

- You can assign two active access keys to a user at a time.

- These can be used to make programmatic calls to AWS when using the **API** in program code or at a command prompt when using the **AWS CLI** or the **AWS PowerShell** tools.

- You can create, modify, view or rotate access keys.

- When created IAM returns the access key ID and secret access key.

- The secret access is returned only at creation time and if lost a new key must be created.

- Ensure access keys and secret access keys are stored securely.

- Users can be given access to change their own keys through IAM policy (not from the console).

- You can disable a user's access key which prevents it from being used for API calls.

Server certificates:

- SSL/TLS certificates that you can use to authenticate with some AWS services.

- AWS recommends that you use the AWS Certificate Manager (ACM) to provision, manage and deploy your server certificates.

- Use IAM only when you must support HTTPS connections in a region that is not supported by ACM.

The following diagram shows the different methods of authentication available with IAM:

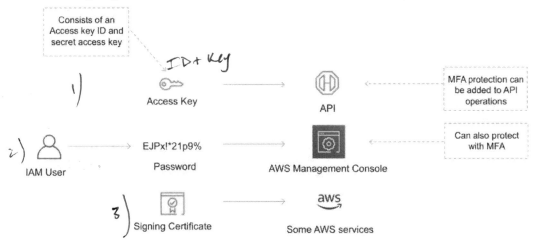

IAM USERS

An IAM user is an entity that represents a person or service.

An IAM user can be assigned:

- An access key ID and secret access key for programmatic access to the AWS API, CLI, SDK, and other development tools.

- A password for access to the management console.

By default, users cannot access anything in your account.

The account root user credentials are the email address used to create the account and a password.

The root account has full administrative permissions and these cannot be restricted.

Best practice for root accounts:

- Don't use the root user credentials

- Don't share the root user credentials

- Create an IAM user and assign administrative permissions as required

- Enable MFA

IAM users can be created to represent applications and these are known as "service accounts".

You can have up to 5,000 users per AWS account.

Each user account has a friendly name and an ARN which uniquely identifies the user across AWS.

A unique ID is also created which is returned only when you create the user using the API, Tools for Windows PowerShell or the AWS CLI.

You should create individual IAM accounts for users (best practice not to share accounts).

The Access Key ID and Secret Access Key are not the same as a password and cannot be used to login to the AWS console.

The Access Key ID and Secret Access Key can only be used once and must be regenerated if lost.

A password policy can be defined for enforcing password length, complexity etc. (applies to all users).

You can allow or disallow the ability to change passwords using an IAM policy.

Access keys and passwords should be changed regularly.

GROUPS

Groups are collections of users and have policies attached to them.

A group is not an identity and cannot be identified as a principal in an IAM policy.

Use groups to assign permissions to users.

Use the principal of least privilege when assigning permissions.

You cannot nest groups (groups within groups).

ROLES

Roles are created and then "assumed" by trusted entities and define a set of permissions for making AWS service requests.

With IAM Roles, you can delegate permissions to resources for users and services without using permanent credentials (e.g., username and password).

IAM users or AWS services can assume a role to obtain temporary security credentials that can be used to make AWS API calls.

You can delegate using roles.

There are no credentials associated with a role (password or access keys).

IAM users can temporarily assume a role to take on permissions for a specific task.

A role can be assigned to a federated user who signs in using an external identity provider.

Temporary credentials are primarily used with IAM roles and automatically expire.

Roles can be assumed temporarily through the console or programmatically with the **AWS CLI, Tools for Windows PowerShell** or **API.**

IAM roles with EC2 instances:

- IAM roles can be used for granting applications running on EC2 instances permissions to AWS API requests using instance profiles.

- Only one role can be assigned to an EC2 instance at a time.

- A role can be assigned at the **EC2 instance creation time or at any time afterwards**.

- When using the AWS CLI or API instance profiles must be created manually (it's automatic and transparent through the console).
- Applications retrieve temporary security credentials from the instance metadata.

Role Delegation:

- Create an IAM role with two policies:
  - Permissions policy – grants the user of the role the required permissions on a resource.
  - Trust policy – specifies the trusted accounts that are allowed to assume the role.
- Wildcards (*) cannot be specified as a principal.
- A permissions policy must also be attached to the user in the trusted account.

POLICIES

JSON → Java Script Notation objint (always)

Policies are documents that define permissions and can be applied to users, groups and roles.

Policy documents are written in JSON (key value pair that consists of an attribute and a value).

All permissions are implicitly denied by default.

The most restrictive policy is applied.

The IAM policy simulator is a tool to help you understand, test, and validate the effects of access control policies.

The Condition element can be used to apply further conditional logic.

AWS SECURITY TOKEN SERVICE (STS)

The AWS Security Token Service (STS) is a web service that enables you to request temporary, limited-privilege credentials for IAM users or for users that you authenticate (federated users).

By default, AWS STS is available as a global service, and all AWS STS requests go to a single endpoint at https://sts.amazonaws.com.

You can optionally send your AWS STS requests to endpoints in any region (can reduce latency).

All regions are enabled for STS by default but can be disabled.

The region in which temporary credentials are requested must be enabled.

Credentials will always work globally.

STS supports AWS CloudTrail, which records AWS calls for your AWS account and delivers log files to an S3 bucket.

Temporary security credentials work almost identically to long-term access key credentials that IAM users can use, with the following differences:

- Temporary security credentials are short-term.
- They can be configured to last anywhere from a few minutes to several hours.

- After the credentials expire, AWS no longer recognizes them or allows any kind of access to API requests made with them.

- Temporary security credentials are not stored with the user but are generated dynamically and provided to the user when requested.

- When (or even before) the temporary security credentials expire, the user can request new credentials, as long as the user requesting them still has permission to do so.

Advantages of STS are:

- You do not have to distribute or embed long-term AWS security credentials with an application.

- You can provide access to your AWS resources to users without having to define an AWS identity for them (temporary security credentials are the basis for IAM Roles and ID Federation).

- The temporary security credentials have a limited lifetime, so you do not have to rotate them or explicitly revoke them when they're no longer needed.

- After temporary security credentials expire, they cannot be reused (you can specify how long the credentials are valid for, up to a maximum limit).

The AWS STS API action returns temporary security credentials that consist of:

- An access key which consists of an access key ID and a secret ID.

- A session token.

- Expiration or duration of validity.

- Users (or an application that the user runs) can use these credentials to access your resources.

With STS you can request a session token using one of the following APIs:

- AssumeRole – can only be used by IAM users (can be used for MFA).

- AssumeRoleWithSAML – can be used by any user who passes a SAML authentication response that indicates authentication from a known (trusted) identity provider.

- AssumeRoleWithWebIdentity – can be used by an user who passes a web identity token that indicates authentication from a known (trusted) identity provider.

- GetSessionToken – can be used by an IAM user or AWS account root user (can be used for MFA).

- GetFederationToken – can be used by an IAM user or AWS account root user.

AWS recommends using Cognito for identity federation with Internet identity providers.

Users can come from three sources.

Federation (typically AD):

- Uses SAML 2.0.

- Grants temporary access based on the users AD credentials.

- Does not need to be a user in IAM.

- Single sign-on allows users to login to the AWS console without assigning IAM credentials.

Federation with Mobile Apps:

- Use Facebook/Amazon/Google or other OpenID providers to login.

Cross Account Access:

- Allows users from one AWS account access resources in another.
- To make a request in a different account the resource in that account must have an attached resource-based policy with the permissions you need.
- Or you must assume a role (identity-based policy) within that account with the permissions you need.

There are a couple of ways STS can be used.

Scenario 1:

- Develop an Identity Broker to communicate with LDAP and AWS STS.
- Identity Broker always authenticates with LDAP first, then with AWS STS.
- Application then gets temporary access to AWS resources.

Scenario 2:

- Develop an Identity Broker to communicate with LDAP and AWS STS.
- Identity Broker authenticates with LDAP first, then gets an IAM role associated with the user.
- Application then authenticates with STS and assumes that IAM role.
- Application uses that IAM role to interact with the service.

IAM BEST PRACTICES

Lock away the AWS root user access keys.

Create individual IAM users.

Use AWS defined policies to assign permissions whenever possible.

Use groups to assign permissions to IAM users.

Grant least privilege.

Use access levels to review IAM permissions.

Configure a strong password policy for users.

Enable MFA for privileged users.

Use roles for applications that run on AWS EC2 instances.

Delegate by using roles instead of sharing credentials.

Rotate credentials regularly.

Remove unnecessary credentials.

Use policy conditions for extra security.

Monitor activity in your AWS account.

Credential Report check:
- Passwords
- Access keys
- MFA

IDENTITY AND ACCESS MANAGEMENT QUIZ QUESTIONS

Answers and explanations are provided below after the last question in this section.

Question 1: An access key ID and secret access key is associated with IAM entity?

A. User   — *person or service*

B. Group

C. Role

D. Policy

Question 2: What are the credentials for an AWS root account?

A. Administrator

B. Root

C. The email address used to create the account   *& pw*

D. The account number

Question 3: What does ARN stand for?

A. Amazon Region Number

B. Amazon Region Name

C. Amazon Resource Number

D. Amazon Resource Name

Question 4: Which principal should be used when assigning permissions to users or groups?

A. Most privilege

B. Least privilege

C. Nesting

D. Most restrictive

Question 5: Which IAM entity can be used to delegate permissions?

A. User

B. Group

C. Role

D. Policy

Question 6: How can you add an extra level of security to your root account?

A. By adding an access key ID and secret access key

B. By adding multi-factor authentication (MFA)

C. By setting a strong password

D. By deleting the root account

Question 7: Which of the following is NOT an IAM security best practice?

✓ A. Use groups to assign permissions to IAM users

✓ B. Configure a strong password policy for users

C. Enable MFA for all users

✓ D. Rotate credentials regularly

Question 8: By default, users are created with what permissions?

A. Full permissions

B. No permissions

C. Minimal permissions

D. No access to the AWS management console

IDENTITY AND ACCESS MANAGEMENT ANSWERS

Question 1, Answer: D

Explanation:

A is incorrect. An access key ID and secret access key is associated with a user and is used for granting programmatic access using the CLI or API.

B is incorrect. You cannot assign an access key ID and secret access key to a group.

C is incorrect. You cannot assign an access key ID and secret access key to a role.

D is correct. You cannot assign an access key ID and secret access key to a policy.

Question 2, Answer: C

Explanation:

A is incorrect. Administrator is not a credential used with AWS.

B is incorrect. root is the username associated with some operating systems such as Linux, it is not an actual username used in your AWS account.

C is correct. The account root user credentials are the email address used to create the account and a password.

D is incorrect. The account number or alias is used to sign in when using an IAM account, rather than the root credentials.

Question 3, Answer: D

Explanation:

A is incorrect. There is no such thing as an Amazon Region Number.

B is incorrect. It does not stand for Amazon Region Name.

C is incorrect. It does not stand for Amazon Resource Number.

D is correct. An Amazon Resource Name (ARN) is associated with entities such as users and groups.

Question 4, Answer: B

Explanation:

A is incorrect. This would be a bad practice as it would provide more privileges to users than they need to perform their jobs.

B is correct. When assigning permissions always grant the least privileges required. This is a security best practice.

C is incorrect. Nesting is not a security practice.

D is incorrect. This would lead to users having too few permissions. You always want to make sure people can perform their jobs whilst not providing too much.

Question 5, Answer: C

Explanation:

A is incorrect. You cannot delegate using users.

B is incorrect. You cannot delegate using Groups, but you can assign permissions to multiple users through groups.

C is correct. You can delegate permissions using roles. It's a great way to provide permissions to resources for users and services without using permanent credentials.

D is incorrect. You cannot delegate using a policy. You delegate using a role and you define permissions to the role through a policy.

Question 6, Answer: B

Explanation:

A is incorrect. No, this will not add security. In fact, it's a security best practice to either remove these from your root account or at least minimize their usage.

B is correct. Adding multi-factor authentication (MFA) to your root account adds an extra level of security as a device is needed to login as well as a username and password. This is a security best practice.

C is incorrect. This is definitely recommended, however this isn't considered an extra level of security.

D is incorrect. You cannot delete the root account.

Question 7, Answer: C

Explanation:

A is incorrect. This is an IAM security best practice.

B is incorrect. This is an IAM security best practice.

C is correct. This is not a security best practice. AWS recommend enabling MFA for all privileged users, but not all users.

D is incorrect. This is an IAM security best practice.

Question 8, Answer: B

Explanation:

A is incorrect. Users are not created with full permissions.

B is correct. Users are created with no permissions. You can then assign permissions using groups and policies.

C is incorrect. Users are not created with minimal permissions, they are created with no permissions.

D is incorrect. Users will have access to the AWS management console, however they won't have any permissions to services by default.

AWS COMPUTE

AMAZON EC2

Amazon Elastic Compute Cloud (Amazon EC2) is a web service in the AWS Compute suite of products that provides secure, resizable compute capacity in the cloud.

The EC2 simple web service interface allows you to obtain and configure capacity with minimal friction.

EC2 is designed to make web-scale cloud computing easier for developers.

Amazon EC2's simple web service interface allows you to obtain and configure capacity with minimal friction.

It provides you with complete control of your computing resources and lets you run on Amazon's proven computing environment.

Amazon EC2 reduces the time required to obtain and boot new server instances to minutes, allowing you to quickly scale capacity, both up and down, as your computing requirements change.

Amazon EC2 changes the economics of computing by allowing you to pay only for capacity that you actually use.

Amazon EC2 provides developers the tools to build failure resilient applications and isolate them from common failure scenarios.

Benefits of EC2 include:

- **Elastic Web-Scale computing** – you can increase or decrease capacity within minutes not hours and commission one to thousands of instances simultaneously.

- **Completely controlled** – You have complete control include root access to each instance and can stop and start instances without losing data and using web service APIs.

- **Flexible Cloud Hosting Services** – you can choose from multiple instance types, operating systems, and software packages as well as instances with varying memory, CPU and storage configurations.

- **Integrated** – EC2 is integrated with most AWS services such as S3, RDS, and VPC to provide a complete, secure solution.

- **Reliable** – EC2 offers a highly reliable environment where replacement instances can be rapidly and predictably commissioned with SLAs of 99.95% for each region.

- **Secure** – EC2 works in conjunction with VPC to provide a secure location with an IP address range you specify and offers Security Groups, Network ACLs, and IPSec VPN features.

- **Inexpensive** – Amazon passes on the financial benefits of scale by charging very low rates and on a capacity consumed basis.

An Amazon Machine Image (AMI) is a special type of virtual appliance that is used to create a virtual machine within the Amazon Elastic Compute Cloud ("EC2").

AMIs come in three main categories:

- **Community AMIs** – free to use, generally you just select the operating system you want.

- **AWS Marketplace AMIs** – pay to use, generally come packaged with additional, licensed software.

- **My AMIs** – AMIs that you create yourself.

Metadata and User Data:

- User data is data that is supplied by the user at instance launch in the form of a script.

- Instance metadata is data about your instance that you can use to configure or manage the running instance.

- User data is limited to 16KB.

- User data and metadata are not encrypted.

- Instance metadata is available at http://169.254.169.254/latest/meta-data

The Instance Metadata Query tool allows you to query the instance metadata without having to type out the full URI or category names.

Pricing

On-demand:

- Good for users that want the low cost and flexibility of EC2 without any up-front payment or long-term commitment.

- Applications with short-term, spiky, or unpredictable workloads that cannot be interrupted.

- Applications being developed or tested on EC2 for the first time.

Reserved:

- Applications with steady state or predictable usage.

- Applications that require reserved capacity.

- Users can make up-front payments to reduce their total computing costs even further.

- Standard Reserved Instances (RIs) provide up to 75% off on-demand price.

- Convertible RIs provide up to 54% off on-demand price – provides the capability to change the attributes of the RI as long as the exchange results in the creation of RIs of equal or greater value.

- Scheduled RIs are available to launch within the time window you reserve. This option allows you to match your capacity reservation to a predictable recurring schedule that only requires a fraction of a day, a week, or a month.

	Standard	Convertible
Terms	1 year, 3 year	1 year, 3 year
Average discount off On-Demand price	40% - 60%	31% - 54%
Change AZ, instance size, networking type	Yes, via ModifyReservedInstance API or console	Yes, via ExchangeReservedInstance API or console
Change instance family, OS, tenancy, payment options	No	Yes
Benefit from price reductions	No	Yes

Spot:

- Applications that have flexible start and end times.
- Applications that are only feasible at very low compute prices.
- Users with an urgent need for a large amount of additional compute capacity.
- If Amazon terminate your instances you do not pay, if you terminate you pay for the hour.

Dedicated hosts:

- Physical servers dedicated just for your use.
- You then have control over which instances are deployed on that host.
- Available as On-Demand or with Dedicated Host Reservation.
- Useful if you have server-bound software licences that use metrics like per-core, per-socket, or per-VM.
- Each dedicated host can only run one EC2 instance size and type.
- Good for regulatory compliance or licensing requirements.
- Predictable performance.
- Complete isolation.
- Most expensive option.
- Billing is per host.

Dedicated instances:

- Virtualized instances on hardware just for you.
- Also uses physically dedicated EC2 servers.
- Does not provide the additional visibility and controls of dedicated hosts (e.g., how instances are placed on a server).

- Billing is per instance.
- May share hardware with other non-dedicated instances in the same account.
- Available as On-Demand, Reserved Instances and Spot Instances.
- Cost additional $2 per hour per region.

The following table describes some of the differences between dedicates instances and dedicated hosts:

Characteristic	Dedicated Instances	Dedicated Hosts
Enables the use of dedicated physical servers	X	X
Per instance billing (subject to a $2 per region fee)	X	
Per host billing		X
Visibility of sockets, cores, host ID		X
Affinity between a host and instance		X
Targeted instance placement		X
Automatic instance placement	X	X
Add capacity using an allocation request		X

Instance Types

Amazon EC2 provides a wide selection of instance types optimized to fit different use cases.

Instance types comprise varying combinations of CPU, memory, storage and networking capacity and give you the flexibility to choose the appropriate mix of resources for your applications.

Each instance type includes one or more instance sizes, allowing you to scale your resources to the requirements of your target workload.

The table below provides an overview of the different EC2 instance types:

Category	Families	Purpose/Design
General Purpose	A1, T3, T3a, T2, M5, M5a, M4	General purpose instances provide a balance of compute, memory and networking resources, and can be used for a variety of diverse workloads
Compute Optimized	C5, C5n, C4	Compute Optimized instances are ideal for compute bound applications that benefit from high performance processors
Memory Optimized	R5, R5a, R4, X1e, X1, High Memory, z1d	Memory optimized instances are designed to deliver fast performance for workloads that process large data sets in memory
Accelerated Compting	P3, P2, G4, G3, F1	Accelerated computing instances use hardware accelerators, or co-processors, to perform functions, such as floating-point number calculations, graphics processing, or data pattern matching
Storage Optimized	I3, I3en, D2, H1	This instance family provides Non-Volatile Memory Express (NVMe) SSD-backed instance storage optimized for low latency, very high random I/O performance, high sequential read throughput and provide high IOPS at a low cost

AMAZON EC2 CONTAINER SERVICE (ECS)

Amazon Elastic Container Service (ECS) is another product in the AWS Compute category. It provides a highly scalable, high performance container management service that supports Docker containers and allows you to easily run applications on a managed cluster of Amazon EC2 instances.

Amazon ECS eliminates the need for you to install, operate, and scale your own cluster management infrastructure.

Using API calls you can launch and stop container-enabled applications, query the complete state of clusters, and access many familiar features like security groups, Elastic Load Balancing, EBS volumes and IAM roles.

Amazon ECS can be used to schedule the placement of containers across clusters based on resource needs and availability requirements.

An Amazon ECS launch type determines the type of infrastructure on which your tasks and services are hosted.

There are two launch types. The table below describes some of the differences between them:

Amazon EC2	Amazon Fargate
You explicitly provision EC2 instances	The control plane asks for resources and Fargate automatically provisions
You're responsible for upgrading, patching, care of EC2 pool	Fargate provisions compute as needed
You must handle cluster optimization	Fargate handles cluster optimization
More granular control over infrastructure	Limited control, as infrastructure is automated

The Elastic container registry (ECR) is a managed AWS Docker registry service for storing, managing and deploying Docker images.

There is no additional charge for Amazon ECS. You pay for AWS resources (e.g., EC2 instances or EBS volumes) you create to store and run your application.

Amazon ECR is integrated with Amazon EC2 Container Service (ECS).

With Amazon ECR, there are no upfront fees or commitments. You pay only for the amount of data you store in your repositories and data transferred to the Internet.

AWS LAMBDA

AWS Lambda is a serverless computing technology that allows you to run code without provisioning or managing servers.

AWS Lambda executes code only when needed and scales automatically.

You pay only for the compute time you consume (you pay nothing when your code is not running).

Benefits of AWS Lambda:

- No servers to manage
- Continuous scaling
- Subsecond metering
- Integrates with almost all other AWS services

Primary use cases for AWS Lambda:

- Data processing
- Real-time file processing
- Real-time stream processing
- Build serverless backends for web, mobile, IOT and 3rd party API requests

AMAZON LIGHTSAIL

AMAZON LIGHTSAIL INSTANCES

Amazon Lightsail is one of the newest services in the AWS Compute suite of products. Amazon Lightsail is great for users who do not have deep AWS technical expertise as it makes it very easy to provision compute services.

Amazon Lightsail provides developers compute, storage and networking capacity and capabilities to deploy and manage websites, web applications and databases in the cloud.

Amazon Lightsail includes everything you need to launch your project quickly – a virtual machine, SSD-based storage, data transfer, DNS management and a static IP.

Amazon Lightsail provides preconfigured virtual private servers (instances) that include everything required to deploy and application or create a database.

The underlying infrastructure and operating system is managed by Amazon Lightsail.

Best suited to projects that require a few dozen instances or fewer.

Provides a simple management interface.

Good for blogs, websites, web applications, e-commerce etc.

Can deploy load balancers and attach block storage.

Public API.

Limited to 20 Amazon Lightsail instances, 5 static IPs, 3 DNS zones, 20 TB block storage, 40 databases, and 5 load balancers per account.

Up to 20 certificates per calendar year.

Can connect to each other and other AWS resources through public Internet and private (VPC peering) networking.

Application templates include WordPress, WordPress Multisite, Drupal, Joomla!, Magento, Redmine, LAMP, Nginx (LEMP), MEAN, Node.js, and more.

Amazon Lightsail currently supports 6 Linux or Unix-like distributions: Amazon Linux, CentOS, Debian, FreeBSD, OpenSUSE, and Ubuntu, as well as 2 Windows Server versions: 2012 R2 and 2016.

AMAZON LIGHTSAIL DATABASES

Amazon Lightsail databases are instances that are dedicated to running databases.

An Amazon Lightsail database can contain multiple user-created databases, and you can access it by using the same tools and applications that you use with a stand-alone database.

Amazon Lightsail managed databases provide an easy, low maintenance way to store your data in the cloud.

Amazon Lightsail manages a range of maintenance activities and security for your database and its underlying infrastructure.

Amazon Lightsail automatically backs up your database and allows point in time restore from the past 7 days using the database restore tool.

Amazon Lightsail databases support the latest major versions of MySQL. Currently, these versions are 5.6, 5.7, and 8.0 for MySQL.

Amazon Lightsail databases are available in Standard and High Availability plans.

High Availability plans add redundancy and durability to your database, by automatically creating standby database in a separate Availability Zone.

Amazon Lightsail is very affordable.

Amazon Lightsail plans are billed on an on-demand hourly rate, so you pay only for what you use.

For every Amazon Lightsail plan you use, you are charged the fixed hourly price, up to the maximum monthly plan cost.

AWS COMPUTE QUIZ QUESTIONS

Answers and explanations are provided below after the last question in this section.

Question 1: What is a benefit of Amazon EC2 compared to traditional servers?

A. You can use specialized hardware

B. You have more control over the operating system

C. You can scale elastically within minutes

D. You get more compute power in the cloud

Question 2: How can you run commands on an Amazon EC2 instance at launch time?

A. With metadata

B. With user data

C. With a container

D. With a snapshot

Question 3: Which service allows you to run Docker containers on AWS?

A. Amazon EC2

B. AWS Lambda

C. Amazon ECS   *EC2 Container Service*

D. Amazon EBS

Question 4: Which of the following services is considered to be a "serverless" service?

A. Amazon EC2

B. Amazon LightSail

C. Amazon ECS with EC2 Launch Type

D. AWS Lambda

Question 5: Which service is good for running compute workloads for people who don't have technical expertise with AWS?

A. Amazon ECS

B. Amazon EC2

C. Amazon LightSail

D. AWS Lambda

Question 6: What are Amazon Machine Images (AMIs) used for?

A. Launching an Amazon EC2 instance

B. Taking a backup of an Amazon EC2 instance

C. Selecting the instance type

D. Running commands at instance launch time

Question 7: Which of the following is NOT a benefit of AWS Lambda?

✓ A. No servers to manage

✓ B. Pay only when your code is running

✓ C. Continuous scaling

D. Multiple instance types to choose from

Question 8: Which storage service is used by Amazon EC2 instances for the root volume?

A. Amazon Simple Storage Service (S3)

B. Amazon Elastic File System (EFS)

C. Amazon Elastic Block Store (EBS)

D. Amazon Storage Gateway

- EC2 - on demand, Reserved, Spot, Dedicate Hosts
  ↓
  Savings Plans   → Not Serveless

- Spot instance termination

, FIGHT DR PKZAU

- EBS - virtual disk

  SSD
  Provisioned IOPS
  General Purpose

  Magnetic
  previous Gen

Linux → SSH
MSFT → Remote Desktop

Security Groups are virtual firewalls

Design for failure
  ↳ one EC2 in each AZ

You can interact w/ AWS in 3 ways:
  1) using the consoles
  2) use Command Line Interface (CLI)
  3) use Software Development Kits (SDKs)

AWS COMPUTE ANSWERS

Question 1, Answer: C

Explanation:

A is incorrect. You cannot use specialized hardware in the cloud. You launch instances on the AWS platform and have no control over the hardware they use.

B is incorrect. You don't have any more control over the operating system in the cloud as in both on-premise and the cloud you have full control.

C is correct. This is a key benefit of the AWS Cloud. You can elastically increase or decrease capacity by changing instance types whenever you need to.

D is incorrect. This is not necessarily true. You can build very powerful compute platforms in your own data center (however it would be very expensive).

Question 2, Answer: B

Explanation:

A is incorrect. Metadata is information about the instance. You can use metadata for finding information such as the availability zone an instance is in or its IP address.

B is correct. User data can be run at instance launch time. You can use it to run commands.

C is incorrect. Containers are another type of compute type, you cannot use a container to run commands on an EC2 instance at launch time.

D is incorrect. Snapshots are copies of EBS volumes that can be used as a backup.

Question 3, Answer: C

Explanation:

A is incorrect. Amazon EC2 is not the service that enables you to use Docker. However, with the EC2 launch type it is used to run the container platform.

B is incorrect. AWS Lambda is used to run functions, not Docker containers.

C is correct. Amazon Elastic Container Service (ECS) is used to run Docker containers on AWS.

D is incorrect. Amazon Elastic Block Store (EBS) is a storage solution that creates "virtual hard drives in the cloud"

Question 4, Answer: D

Explanation:

A is incorrect. With Amazon EC2, you must manage the instances you provision.

B is incorrect. With Amazon LigthtSail, you must manage the instances you provision.

C is incorrect. With the EC2 launch type, you must manage the Amazon EC2 container instances.

D is correct. AWS Lambda is a serverless services that runs code as "functions".

Question 5, Answer: C

Explanation

A is incorrect. Managing Amazon ECS requires good technical knowledge of AWS.

B is incorrect. Managing Amazon EC2 requires good technical knowledge of AWS.

C is correct. Amazon LightSail is great for users who do not have deep AWS technical expertise as it make it very easy to provision compute services.

D is incorrect. Managing AWS Lambda requires good technical knowledge of AWS.

Question 6, Answer: A

Explanation:

A is correct. An Amazon Machine Image (AMI) provides the information required to launch an instance.

B is incorrect. You use snapshots to take a backup of an EC2 instance (or more correctly, its EBS volume).

C is incorrect. You don't use an AMI to select an instance type. You choose your AMI, then choose your instance type.

D is incorrect. You use user data to run commands at instance launch time.

Question 7, Answer: D

Explanation:

A is incorrect. This is a benefit of AWS Lambda - there are no servers to manage which is why it is known as a "serverless" service.

B is incorrect. You do only pay when your code is running and this is a great benefit of AWS Lambda.

C is incorrect. AWS Lambda includes continuous scaling which means it elastically adjusts to demand.

D is correct. As AWS Lambda is a serverless service, there are no instance types to choose from.

Question 8, Answer: C

Explanation:

A is incorrect. Amazon S3 is an object-based storage system and is not used for EC2 root volumes.

B is incorrect. Amazon Elastic File System (EFS) is a file-based storage service. You can mount EFS filesystems to an EC2 instance but you cannot use them for root volumes

C is correct. Amazon Elastic Block Store (EBS) is used for the root volume on EBS-backed instances.

D is incorrect. Amazon Storage Gateway is a storage solution used for hybrid storage between on-premises and AWS Cloud.

AWS STORAGE

AMAZON SIMPLE STORAGE SERVICE (S3)

Amazon S3 is object storage built to store and retrieve any amount of data from anywhere – web sites and mobile apps, corporate applications and data from IoT sensors or devices.

You can store any type of file in S3. → *flat files, don't change*

S3 is designed to deliver 99.999999999% durability, and stores data for millions of applications used by market leaders in every industry.

S3 provides comprehensive security and compliance capabilities that meet even the most stringent regulatory requirements.

S3 gives customers flexibility in the way they manage data for cost optimization, access control, and compliance.

Typical use cases include:

- Backup and Storage – Provide data backup and storage services for others.
- Application Hosting – Provide services that deploy, install, and manage web applications.
- Media Hosting – Build a redundant, scalable, and highly available infrastructure that hosts video, photo, or music uploads and downloads.
- Software Delivery – Host your software applications that customers can download.
- Static Website – you can configure a static website to run from an S3 bucket.

S3 provides query-in-place functionality, allowing you to run powerful analytics directly on your data at rest in S3. And Amazon S3 is the most supported cloud storage service available, with integration from the largest community of third-party solutions, systems integrator partners, and other AWS services.

Files can be anywhere from 0 bytes to 5 TB.

There is unlimited storage available.

Files are stored in buckets.

Buckets are root level folders.

Any subfolder within a bucket is known as a "folder".

S3 is a universal namespace so bucket names must be unique globally.

There are six S3 storage classes.

- S3 Standard (durable, immediately available, frequently accessed)
- S3 Intelligent-Tiering (automatically moves data to the most cost-effective tier)
- S3 Standard-IA (durable, immediately available, infrequently accessed)
- S3 One Zone-IA (lower cost for infrequently accessed data with less resilience)
- S3 Glacier (archived data, retrieval times in minutes or hours)

- S3 Glacier Deep Archive (lowest cost storage class for long term retention)

The table below provides the details of each Amazon S3 storage class:

	S3 Standard	S3 Intelligent-Tiering*	S3 Standard-IA	S3 One Zone-IA†	S3 Glacier	S3 Glacier Deep Archive
Designed for durability	99.999999999% (11 9's)	99.999999999% (11 9's)	99.999999999% (11 9's)	99.999999999% (11 9's)	99.999999999% (11 9's)	99.999999999% (11 9's)
Designed for availability	99.99%	99.9%	99.9%	99.5%	99.99%	99.99%
Availability SLA	99.9%	99%	99%	99%	99.9%	99.9%
Availability Zones	≥3	≥3	≥3	1	≥3	≥3
Minimum capacity charge per object	N/A	N/A	128KB	128KB	40KB	40KB
Minimum storage duration charge	N/A	30 days	30 days	30 days	90 days	180 days
Retrieval fee	N/A	N/A	per GB retrieved	per GB retrieved	per GB retrieved	per GB retrieved
First byte latency	milliseconds	millseconds	milliseconds	milliseconds	select minutes or hours	select hours
Storage type	Object	Object	Object	Object	Object	Object
Lifecycle transitions	Yes	Yes	Yes	Yes	Yes	Yes

When you successfully upload a file to S3 you receive a HTTP 200 code. *Exam*

S3 is a persistent, highly durable data store.

Persistent data stores are non-volatile storage systems that retain data when powered off.

This is in contrast to transient data stores and ephemeral data stores which lose the data when powered off.

The following table provides a description of persistent, transient and ephemeral data stores and which AWS service to use:

Storage Type	Description	Examples
Persistent Data Store	Data is durable and sticks around after reboots, restarts, or power cycles	S3, Glacier, EBS, EFS
Transient Data Store	Data is just temporarily stored and passed along to another process or persistent store	SQS, SNS
Ephemeral Data Store	Data is lost when the system is stopped	EC2 Instance Store, Memcached

Bucket names must follow a set of rules:

- Names must be unique across all of AWS.
- Names must be 3 to 63 characters in length.
- Names can only contain lowercase letters, numbers and hyphens.
- Names cannot be formatted as an IP address.

Data consistency:

- "Read after write" consistency for PUTS of new objects.
- "Eventual consistency" for overwrite PUTS and DELETES (takes time to propagate).

) Exam

Objects consist of:

- Key (name of the object).
- Value (data made up of a sequence of bytes).
- Version ID (used for versioning).
- Metadata (data about the data that is stored).

) Exam

Subresources:

- Access control lists
- Torrent

Built for 99.99 availability.

SLA is 99.9% availability.

Amazon guarantee 99.99999999% durability.   *11x 9s*

Object sharing – the ability to make any object publicly available via a URL.

Lifecycle management – set rules to transfer objects between storage classes at defined time intervals.

Versioning – automatically keep multiple versions of an object (when enabled).

Encryption.

Data secured using ACLs and bucket policies.

Tiers:

- S3 standard
- S3-IA   *Infrequent Access*
- S3 One Zone – IA   *(non – multiple AZs)*
- Glacier   *– AI-based optimization*

Charges:

- Storage   *(per GB)*
- Request
- Storage management pricing

- Data transfer pricing
- Transfer acceleration

When you create a bucket, you need to select the region where it will be created.

It is a best practice to create buckets in regions that are physically closest to your users to reduce latency.

Additional capabilities offered by Amazon S3 include:

Additional S3 Capability	How it Works
Transfer Acceleration	Speed up data uploads using CloudFront in reverse
Requester Pays	The requester rather than the bucket owner pays for requests and data transfer
Tags	Assign tags to objects to use in costing, billing, security etc.
Events	Trigger notifications to SNS, SQS, or Lambda when certain events happen in your bucket
Static Web Hosting	Simple and massively scalable static website hosting
BitTorrent	Use the BitTorrent protocol to retrieve any publicly available object by automatically generating a .torrent file

AWS SNOWBALL

With AWS Snowball (Snowball), you can transfer hundreds of terabytes or petabytes of data between your on-premises data centers and Amazon Simple Storage Service (Amazon S3).

Uses a secure storage device for physical transportation.

AWS Snowball Client is software that is installed on a local computer and is used to identify, compress, encrypt, and transfer data.

Uses 256-bit encryption (managed with the AWS KMS) and tamper-resistant enclosures with TPM.

Snowball (80TB) 50TB model available only in the USA.

Snowball Edge (100TB) comes with onboard storage and compute capabilities.

Snowmobile – exabyte scale with up to 100PB per Snowmobile.

Snowball can import to S3 or export from S3.

Import/export is when you send your own disks into AWS – this is being deprecated in favor of Snowball.

Snowball must be ordered from and returned to the same region.

To speed up data transfer it is recommended to run simultaneous instances of the AWS Snowball Client in multiple terminals and transfer small files as batches.

AMAZON ELASTIC BLOCK STORE (EBS)

think EBS *Virtual Hard disk in the Cloud*

Amazon Elastic Block Store (Amazon EBS) provides persistent block storage volumes for use with Amazon EC2 instances in the AWS Cloud.

Each Amazon EBS volume is automatically replicated within its Availability Zone to protect you from component failure, offering high availability and durability.

Amazon EBS volumes offer the consistent and low-latency performance needed to run your workloads. With Amazon EBS, you can scale your usage up or down within minutes – all while paying a low price for only what you provision.

Databases & OS

The following table shows a comparison of a few **EBS volume types**:

	Solid State Drives (SSD)		Hard Disk Drives (HDD)	
Volume Type	EBS Provisioned IOPS SSD (io1)	EBS General Purpose SSD (gp2)*	Throughput Optimized HDD (st1)	Cold HDD (sc1)
Short Description	Highest performance SSD volume designed for latency-sensitive transactional workloads	General Purpose SSD volume that balances price performance for a wide variety of transactional workloads	Low cost HDD volume designed for frequently accessed, throughput intensive workloads	Lowest cost HDD volume designed for less frequently accessed workloads
Use Cases	I/O-intensive NoSQL and relational databases	Boot volumes, low-latency interactive apps, dev & test	Big data, data warehouses, log processing	Colder data requiring fewer scans per day
API Name	io1	gp2	st1	sc1
Volume Size	4 GB - 16 TB	1 GB - 16 TB	500 GB - 16 TB	500 GB - 16 TB
Max IOPS**/Volume	64,000	16,000	500	250
Max Throughput***/Volume	1,000 MB/s	250 MB/s	500 MB/s	250 MB/s
Max IOPS/Instance	80,000	80,000	80,000	80,000
Max Throughput/Instance	1,750 MB/s	1,750 MB/s	1,750 MB/s	1,750 MB/s

EBS volume data persists independently of the life of the instance.

EBS volumes do not need to be attached to an instance.

You can attach multiple EBS volumes to an instance.

You cannot attach an EBS volume to multiple instances (use Elastic File Store instead).

EBS volumes must be in the same AZ as the instances they are attached to.

Termination protection is turned off by default and must be manually enabled (keeps the volume/data when the instance is terminated).

Root EBS volumes are deleted on termination by default.

Extra non-boot volumes are not deleted on termination by default.

The behavior can be changed by altering the "DeleteOnTermination" attribute.

EBS Snapshots:

- Snapshots capture a point-in-time state of an instance.

- Snapshots are stored on S3.

- Does not provide granular backup (not a replacement for backup software).

- If you make periodic snapshots of a volume, the snapshots are incremental, which means that only the blocks on the device that have changed after your last snapshot are saved in the new snapshot.

- Even though snapshots are saved incrementally, the snapshot deletion process is designed so that you need to retain only the most recent snapshot in order to restore the volume.

- Snapshots can only be accessed through the EC2 APIs.

- EBS volumes are AZ specific but snapshots are region specific.

INSTANCE STORES

Instance store volumes are high performance local disks that are physically attached to the host computer on which an EC2 instance runs.

Instance stores are ephemeral which means the data is lost when powered off (non-persistent).

Instances stores are ideal for temporary storage of information that changes frequently, such as buffers, caches, or scratch data.

Instance store volume root devices are created from AMI templates stored on S3.

Instance store volumes cannot be detached/reattached.

AMAZON ELASTIC FILE SERVICE (EFS) ← Elastic, arbo

EFS is a fully managed service that makes it easy to set up and scale file storage in the Amazon Cloud.

Good for big data and analytics, media processing workflows, content management, web serving, home directories, etc.

EFS uses the NFSv4.1 protocol.

Pay for what you use (no pre-provisioning required).

Can scale up to petabytes.

EFS is elastic and grows and shrinks as you add and remove data.

Can concurrently connect 1 to 1000s of EC2 instances, from multiple AZs.

A file system can be accessed concurrently from all AZs in the region where it is located.

By default, you can create up to 10 file systems per account.

On-premises access can be enabled via Direct Connect or AWS VPN.

Can choose General Purpose or Max I/O (both SSD).

The VPC of the connecting instance must have DNS hostnames enabled.

EFS provides a file system interface, file system access semantics (such as strong consistency and file locking).

Data is stored across multiple AZ's within a region.

Read after write consistency.

Need to create mount targets and choose AZ's to include (recommended to include all AZ's).

Instances can be behind an ELB.

There are two performance modes:

- "General Purpose" performance mode is appropriate for most file systems.
- "Max I/O" performance mode is optimized for applications where tens, hundreds, or thousands of EC2 instances are accessing the file system.

Amazon EFS is designed to burst to allow high throughput levels for periods of time.

Exam:

- S3 is Object-based; allows you to upload files
- Files can be from 0 bytes to 5TB
- Unlimited Storage
- Files are stored in buckets
- S3 is a universal namespace → all names must be different
- https://s3region/name
- Not suitable for OS or DB storage

- "Key value" pairs
- Eventual consistency — PUTS, PUTS & Deletes
- Storage types (6)

AWS STORAGE QUIZ QUESTIONS

Answers and explanations are provided below after the last question in this section.

Question 1: Amazon S3 is an example of what type of storage system?

A. Object

B. Block ~ *EBS*

C. File ~ *EFS*

D. Hybrid

Question 2: With Amazon S3, objects are stored in which type of root-level container?

A. A folder

B. A file-system

C. A bucket

D. A region

Question 3: Amazon Elastic Block Store (EBS) volumes are stored within which construct?

A. A region

B. An edge location

C. A snapshot

D. An availability zone

Question 4: Which storage service can be used on-premises to access cloud storage?

A. Amazon S3 Glacier

B. Amazon Storage Block

C. AWS Storage Gateway   *gateway = on prem*

D. AWS Hybrid Service

Question 5: With default settings, what will happen to a root EBS volume when the Amazon EC2 instance is terminated?

A. It will be deleted

B. It will be retained   ~ *op many*

C. A snapshot will be retained ~ *op many*

D. An AMI will be created

Question 6: Which Amazon Machine Image can be used to mount an Amazon Elastic File System (EFS) file system?

A. Microsoft Windows Server 2019 with Containers

B. Microsoft Windows Server 2016 Core

C. Amazon Linux 2 AMI

D. All of the above

Question 7: Which storage device is physically attached to the Amazon EC2 host servers?

A. Amazon Elastic Block Store (EBS) volume

B. Amazon Machine Image (AMI)

C. Instance Store volume

D. Elastic Network Adapter

Question 8: Which Amazon S3 storage class is used for archiving data for long term retention?

A. S3 Standard

B. S3 Intelligent-Tiering

C. S3 One Zone-IA

D. S3 Glacier Deep Archive

Restricting Bucket Access

• Bucket policies - applies across the whole bucket
• Object policies - applies to ind. files
• IAM Policies : User Groups - applies to U. & G.

You can use bucket policies to make entire S3 buckets public

S3 can host static websites

S3 scales automatically

Versioning

AWS STORAGE ANSWERS

Question 1, Answer: A

Explanation:

A is correct. Amazon Simple Storage Service (S3) is an object-based storage system.

B is incorrect. Amazon Simple Storage Service (S3) is not a block-based storage system.

C is incorrect. Amazon Simple Storage Service (S3) is not a file-based storage system.

D is incorrect. Amazon Simple Storage Service (S3) is not a hybrid storage system. An example of a hybrid storage system would be Amazon Storage Gateway.

Question 2, Answer: C

Explanation:

A is incorrect. You can create folders with Amazon S3 to mimic a hierarchy but they are not root-level containers.

B is incorrect. Amazon S3 is an object-based storage system, there is no such thing as a file-system.

C is correct. A bucket is the root-level container in Amazon S3. You upload your objects into buckets

D is incorrect. A region is not the root-level container in Amazon S3. Buckets are created within a region.

Question 3, Answer: D

Explanation:

A is incorrect. Amazon EBS volumes are not stored within a region. They are stored within another construct that is within a region. Guess again!

B is incorrect. An edge location is not where you store EBS volumes. Edge Locations are used by the Amazon CloudFront service and will be discussed later in the course.

C is incorrect. You don't store an Amazon EBS volume in a snapshot, you take snapshots of EBS volumes to get point-in-time backups of the data in the volume.

D is correct. Amazon EBS volumes are stored with an availability zone.

Question 4, Answer: C

Explanation:

A is incorrect. Amazon S3 Glacier is a cloud storage solution used for archiving data.

B is incorrect. There's no such thing as "Amazon Storage Block".

C is correct. AWS Storage Gateway is a hybrid cloud storage service that gives you on-premises access to virtually unlimited cloud storage.

D is incorrect. There's no such thing as "AWS Hybrid Service".

Question 5, Answer: A

Explanation:

A is correct. With default settings an Amazon EBS root volume will be deleted when the instance is terminated.

B is incorrect. This is, not true with default settings. However, you can configure EBS volumes to be retained by changing the "Delete on termination" attribute.

C is incorrect. A snapshot is not automatically created when an instance is terminated.

D is incorrect. An AMI will not be created.

Question 6, Answer: C

Explanation:

A is incorrect. You cannot use Microsoft Windows AMIs with Amazon EFS.

B is incorrect. You cannot use Microsoft Windows AMIs with Amazon EFS.

C is incorrect. Only Linux AMIs can be used with Amazon EFS.

D is incorrect. You cannot use Microsoft Windows AMIs with Amazon EFS.

Question 7, Answer: C

Explanation:

A is incorrect. Amazon EBS volumes are attached over a network, they are not physically attached to the EC2 host servers.

B is incorrect. An AMI is used to launch an instance, it is not a storage device.

C is correct. Instance store volumes are physically attached to EC2 host servers. They are ephemeral storage which means the data is lost when powered off.

D is incorrect. An ENA is not a storage device.

Question 8, Answer: D

Explanation:

A is incorrect. S3 Standard is durable, immediately available, frequently accessed storage.

B is incorrect. S3 Intelligent-Tiering automatically moves data to the most cost-effective tier.

C is incorrect. S3 One Zone-IA is lower cost storage for infrequently accessed data with less resilience.

D is correct. S3 Glacier Deep Archive is the lowest cost storage class for long term retention.

AWS NETWORKING

GENERAL AMAZON VIRTUAL PRIVATE CLOUD (VPC) = DC

A virtual private cloud (VPC) is a virtual network dedicated to your AWS account.

Analogous to having your own Data Centre (DC) inside AWS.

It is logically isolated from other virtual networks in the AWS Cloud.

Provides complete control over the virtual networking environment including selection of IP ranges, creation of subnets and configuration of route tables and gateways.

You can launch your AWS resources, such as Amazon EC2 instances, into your VPC.

When you create a VPC, you must specify a range of IPv4 addresses for the VPC in the form of a Classless Inter-Domain Routing (CIDR) block; e.g. 10.0.0.0/16.

This is the primary CIDR block for your VPC.

A VPC spans all the Availability Zones in the region.

You have full control over who has access to the AWS resources inside your VPC.

You can create your own IP address ranges, and create subnets, route tables and network gateways.

When you first create your AWS account a default VPC is created for you in each AWS region.

A default VPC is created in each region with a subnet in each AZ.

By default, you can create up to 5 VPCs per region.

You can define dedicated tenancy for a VPC to ensure instances are launched on dedicated hardware (overrides the configuration specified at launch).

A default VPC is automatically created for each AWS account the first time Amazon EC2 resources are provisioned.

The default VPC has all-public subnets.

Public subnets are subnets that have:

- "Auto-assign public IPv4 address" set to "Yes"
- The subnet route table has an attached Internet Gateway

Instances in the default VPC always have both a public and private IP address.

AZs names are mapped to different zones for different users (i.e. the AZ "ap-southeast-2a" may map to a different physical zone for a different user).

Components of a VPC:

- **A Virtual Private Cloud**: A logically isolated virtual network in the AWS cloud. You define a VPC's IP address space from ranges you select.

- **Subnet**: A segment of a VPC's IP address range where you can place groups of isolated resources (maps to an AZ, 1:1).

- **Internet Gateway**: The Amazon VPC side of a connection to the public Internet.

- **NAT Gateway**: A highly available, managed Network Address Translation (NAT) service for your resources in a private subnet to access the Internet.
- **Hardware VPN Connection**: A hardware-based VPN connection between your Amazon VPC and your datacenter, home network, or co-location facility.
- **Virtual Private Gateway**: The Amazon VPC side of a VPN connection.
- **Customer Gateway**: Your side of a VPN connection.
- **Router**: Routers interconnect subnets and direct traffic between Internet gateways, virtual private gateways, NAT gateways, and subnets.
- **Peering Connection**: A peering connection enables you to route traffic via private IP addresses between two peered VPCs.
- **VPC Endpoints**: Enables private connectivity to services hosted in AWS, from within your VPC without using an Internet Gateway, VPN, Network Address Translation (NAT) devices, or firewall proxies.
- **Egress-only Internet Gateway**: A stateful gateway to provide egress only access for IPv6 traffic from the VPC to the Internet.

Options for securely connecting to a VPC are:

- AWS managed VPN – fast to setup
- Direct Connect – high bandwidth, low-latency but takes weeks to months to setup
- VPN CloudHub – used for connecting multiple sites to AWS
- Software VPN – use 3rd party software

An Elastic Network Interface (ENI) is a logical networking component that represents a NIC.

ENIs can be attached and detached from EC2 instances and the configuration of the ENI will be maintained.

Flow Logs capture information about the IP traffic going to and from network interfaces in a VPC.

Flow log data is stored using Amazon CloudWatch Logs.

Flow logs can be created at the following levels:

- VPC
- Subnet
- Network interface

Peering connections can be created with VPCs in different regions (available in most regions now).

Data sent between VPCs in different regions is encrypted (traffic charges apply).

SUBNETS

After creating a VPC, you can add one or more subnets in each Availability Zone.

When you create a subnet, you specify the CIDR block for the subnet, which is a subset of the VPC CIDR block.

Each subnet must reside entirely within one Availability Zone and cannot span zones.

Types of subnet:

- If a subnet's traffic is routed to an internet gateway, the subnet is known as a public subnet.

- If a subnet doesn't have a route to the internet gateway, the subnet is known as a private subnet.

- If a subnet doesn't have a route to the internet gateway, but has its traffic routed to a virtual private gateway for a VPN connection, the subnet is known as a VPN-only subnet.

An Internet Gateway is a horizontally scaled, redundant, and highly available VPC component that allows communication between instances in your VPC and the internet.

FIREWALLS

Network Access Control Lists (ACLs) provide a firewall/security layer at the subnet level.

Security Groups provide a firewall/security layer at the instance level.

The table below describes some differences between Security Groups and Network ACLs:

Security Group	Network ACL
Operates at the instance (interface) level	Operates at the subnet level
Supports allow rules only	Supports allow and deny rules
Stateful	Stateless
Evaluates all rules	Processes rules in order
Applies to an instance only if associated with a group	Automatically applies to all instances in the subnets its associated with

VPC WIZARD

The VPC Wizard can be used to create the following four configurations:

VPC with a Single Public Subnet:

- Your instances run in a private, isolated section of the AWS cloud with direct access to the Internet.

- Network access control lists and security groups can be used to provide strict control over inbound and outbound network traffic to your instances.

- Creates a /16 network with a /24 subnet. Public subnet instances use Elastic IPs or Public IPs to access the Internet.

VPC with Public and Private Subnets:

- In addition to containing a public subnet, this configuration adds a private subnet whose instances are not addressable from the Internet.

- Instances in the private subnet can establish outbound connections to the Internet via the public subnet using Network Address Translation (NAT).

- Creates a /16 network with two /24 subnets.

- Public subnet instances use Elastic IPs to access the Internet.

- Private subnet instances access the Internet via Network Address Translation (NAT).

3 **VPC with Public and Private Subnets and Hardware VPN Access:**

- This configuration adds an IPsec Virtual Private Network (VPN) connection between your Amazon VPC and your data center – effectively extending your data center to the cloud while also providing direct access to the Internet for public subnet instances in your Amazon VPC.

- Creates a /16 network with two /24 subnets.

- One subnet is directly connected to the Internet while the other subnet is connected to your corporate network via an IPsec VPN tunnel.

4 **VPC with a Private Subnet Only and Hardware VPN Access:**

- Your instances run in a private, isolated section of the AWS cloud with a private subnet whose instances are not addressable from the Internet.

- You can connect this private subnet to your corporate data center via an IPsec Virtual Private Network (VPN) tunnel.

- Creates a /16 network with a /24 subnet and provisions an IPsec VPN tunnel between your Amazon VPC and your corporate network.

NAT INSTANCES

NAT instances are managed **by** you.

Used to enable private subnet instances to access the Internet.

When creating NAT instances always disable the source/destination check on the instance.

NAT instances must be in a single public subnet.

NAT instances need to be assigned to security groups.

NAT GATEWAYS

NAT gateways are **managed for you** by AWS.

NAT gateways are highly available in each AZ into which they are deployed.

They are preferred by enterprises.

Can scale automatically up to 45Gbps.

No need to patch.

Not associated with any security groups.

The table below describes some **differences between NAT instances and NAT gateways**:

NAT Instance	NAT Gateway
Managed by you (e.g. software updates)	Managed by AWS
Scale up (instance type) manually and use enhanced networking	Elastic scalability up to 45 Gbps
No high availability – scripted/auto-scaled HA possible using multiple NATs in multiple subnets	Provides automatic high availability within an AZ and can be placed in multiple AZs
Need to assign Security Group	No Security Groups
Can use as a bastion host	Cannot access through SSH
Use an Elastic IP address or a public IP address with a NAT instance	Choose the Elastic IP address to associate with a NAT gateway at creation
Can implement port forwarding through manual customisation	Does not support port forwarding

AWS DIRECT CONNECT

AWS Direct Connect is a network service that provides an alternative to using the Internet to connect a customer's on-premise sites to AWS.

Data is transmitted through a private network connection between AWS and a customer's datacenter or corporate network.

Benefits:

- Reduce cost when using large volumes of traffic
- Increase reliability (predictable performance)
- Increase bandwidth (predictable bandwidth)
- Decrease latency

Each AWS Direct Connect connection can be configured with one or more virtual interfaces (VIFs).

Public VIFs allow access to public services such as S3, EC2 and DynamoDB.

Private VIFs allow access to your VPC.

From Direct Connect you can **connect to all AZs within the region.**

You can establish IPSec connections over public VIFs to remote regions.

Direct Connect is charged by port hours and data transfer.

Available in 1Gbps and 10Gbps.

Speeds of 50Mbps, 100Mbps, 200Mbps, 300Mbps, 400Mbps, and 500Mbps can be purchased through AWS Direct Connect Partners.

Uses Ethernet trunking (802.1q).

Each connection consists of a single dedicated connection between ports on the customer router and an Amazon router.

For HA you must have 2 DX connections – can be active/active or active/standby.

Route tables need to be updated to point to a Direct Connect connection.

VPN can be maintained as a backup with a higher BGP priority.

You cannot extend your on-premise VLANs into the AWS cloud using Direct Connect.

AWS NETWORKING QUIZ QUESTIONS

Answers and explanations are provided below after the last question in this section.

Question 1: What is the scope of an Amazon VPC?

A. A data center

B. A region

C. An availability zone

D. A subnet

Question 2: Which type of firewall operates at the instance level?

A. A security group

B. A network access control list (NACL)

C. A route table

D. A NAT Gateway

Question 3: How can an organization create a private hybrid cloud connection between their on-premises data center and the AWS Cloud?

A. AWS managed VPN

B. VPN CloudHub

C. Software VPN

D. AWS Direct Connect

Question 4: Which type of public IP address is retained when the instance is stopped?

A. Public IP address

B. Private IP address

C. Elastic IP address

D. Local IP address

Question 5: Which AWS-managed network service can be used to enable Internet connectivity for EC2 instances in private subnets?

A. NAT Instance

B. NAT Gateway

C. Internet Gateway

D. Network ACL

Question 6: A company needs a network connection to the AWS cloud with predictable performance. What should they use?

A. AWS managed VPN

B. AWS Direct Connect

C. VPN CloudHub

D. VPC Peering

AWS NETWORKING ANSWERS

Question 1, Answer: B

Explanation:

A is incorrect. The scope of a VPC is not a data center. AWS never talk in terms of data centers as these are transparent to the user.

B is correct. An Amazon VPC is created within a region. You can create multiple VPCs within a region and there is a default VPC created in every AWS region by default.

C is incorrect. You do not create VPC's within availability zones. AZs are actually constructs to which you assign subnets within your VPC.

D is incorrect. A subnet is assigned to an availability zone, you don't create a VPC in a subnet.

Question 2, Answer: A

Explanation:

A is correct. Security groups are considered to be instance-level firewalls.

B is incorrect. A network access control list or NACL is a subnet-level firewall.

C is incorrect. A route table is not a firewall. It is used to direct network traffic.

D is incorrect. A NAT Gateway is not a firewall. It is used to provide Internet access to EC2 instances in private subnets.

Question 3, Answer: 4

Explanation:

A is incorrect. A virtual private network (VPN) is a connection over the public Internet and is therefore not considered private.

B is incorrect. A virtual private network (VPN) is a connection over the public Internet and is therefore not considered private.

C is incorrect. A virtual private network (VPN) is a connection over the public Internet and is therefore not considered private.

D is correct. AWS Direct Connect is a private network connection to the AWS Cloud. It provides high bandwidth and low latency with reliable performance.

Question 4, Answer: C

Explanation:

A is incorrect. Public IP addresses are lost when the instance is stopped.

B is incorrect. A private IP address is not a public IP address.

C is correct. With Elastic IP addresses, the address is retained when the instance is stopped. Remember that you do pay for unused Elastic IP addresses.

D is incorrect. This is not a type of Public IP address.

Question 5, Answer: B

Explanation:

A is incorrect. A NAT instance is an EC2 instance managed by you that can be used for enabling instance in private subnets to access the Internet.

B is correct. A NAT Gateway is an AWS managed service that can be used for enabling instance in private subnets to access the Internet.

C is incorrect. An Internet Gateway is attached to a VPC to enable Internet connectivity. However, you need a NAT Instance or NAT Gateway to enable instance in private subnets to access the Internet using the Internet Gateway.

D is incorrect. A network ACL is a subnet-level firewall.

Question 6, Answer: B

Explanation:

A is incorrect. Because a VPN uses the public Internet, it doesn't offer predictable performance.

B is correct. AWS Direct Connect is a private network connection and offers predictable performance.

C is incorrect. Because a VPN uses the public Internet, it doesn't offer predictable performance.

D is incorrect. VPC Peering is a method of connecting two VPCs together, not for connecting into AWS from an organization.

AWS DATABASES

USE CASES FOR DIFFERENT DATABASE TYPES

The table below provides guidance on the typical use cases for several AWS database/data store services:

Data Store	When to Use
Database on EC2	• Ultimate control over database • Preferred DB not available under RDS
Amazon RDS	• Need traditional relational database for OLTP • Your data is well-formed and structured • Existing apps requiring RDBMS
Amazon DynamoDB	• Name/value pair data or unpredictable data structure • In-memory performance with persistence • High I/O needs • Scale dynamically
Amazon RedShift	• Massive amounts of data • Primarily OLAP workloads
Amazon Neptune	• Relationships between objects a major portion of data value
Amazon ElastiCache	• Fast temporary storage for small amounts of data • Highly volatile data
Amazon S3	• BLOBs • Static websites

We'll now cover several of these database types that may come up on the exam.

AMAZON RELATIONAL DATABASE SERVICES (RDS)

Amazon Relational Database Service (Amazon RDS) is a managed service that makes it easy to set up, operate and scale a relational database in the cloud.

Relational databases are known as Structured Query Language (SQL) databases.

Non-relational databases are known as NoSQL databases.

RDS is an Online Transaction Processing (OLTP) type of database.

RDS features and benefits:

- SQL type of database
- Can be used to perform complex queries and joins
- Easy to setup, highly available, fault tolerant and scalable
- Used when data is clearly defined
- Common use cases include online stores and banking systems

Amazon RDS supports the following database engines:

- SQL Server
- Oracle
- MySQL Server
- PostgreSQL
- Aurora
- MariaDB

Aurora is Amazon's proprietary database.

RDS is a fully managed service and you do not have access to the underlying EC2 instance (no root access).

The RDS service includes the following:

- Security and patching of the DB instances
- Automated backup for the DB instances
- Software updates for the DB engine
- Easy scaling for storage and compute
- Multi-AZ option with synchronous replication
- Automatic failover for Multi-AZ option
- Read replicas option for read heavy workloads

A DB instance is a database environment in the cloud with the compute and storage resources you specify.

Encryption:

- You can encrypt your Amazon RDS instances and snapshots at rest by enabling the encryption option for your Amazon RDS DB instance.
- Encryption at rest is supported for all DB types and uses AWS KMS.
- You cannot encrypt an existing DB. You need to create a snapshot, copy it, encrypt the copy, then build an encrypted DB from the snapshot.

DB Subnet Groups:

- A DB subnet group is a collection of subnets (typically private) that you create in a VPC and that you then designate for your DB instances.

- Each DB subnet group should have subnets in at least two Availability Zones in a given region.
- It is recommended to configure a subnet group with subnets in each AZ (even for standalone instances).

AWS Charge for:

- DB instance hours (partial hours are charged as full hours)
- Storage GB/month
- I/O requests/month – for magnetic storage
- Provisioned IOPS/month – for RDS provisioned IOPS SSD
- Egress data transfer
- Backup storage (DB backups and manual snapshots)

Scalability:

- You can only scale RDS up (compute and storage)
- You cannot decrease the allocated storage for an RDS instance
- You can scale storage and change the storage type for all DB engines except MS SQL

RDS provides multi-AZ for disaster recovery which provides fault tolerance across availability zones:

- Multi-AZ RDS creates a replica in another AZ and synchronously replicates to it (DR only).
- There is an option to choose multi-AZ during the launch wizard.
- AWS recommends the use of provisioned IOPS storage for multi-AZ RDS DB instances.
- Each AZ runs on its own physically distinct, independent infrastructure, and is engineered to be highly reliable.
- You cannot choose which AZ in the region will be chosen to create the standby DB instance.

Read Replicas – provide improved performance for reads:

- Read replicas are used for read heavy DBs and replication is asynchronous.
- Read replicas are for workload sharing and offloading.
- Read replicas provide read-only DR.
- Read replicas are created from a snapshot of the master instance.
- Must have automated backups enabled on the primary (retention period > 0).

AMAZON DYNAMODB

Amazon DynamoDB is a fully managed NoSQL database service that provides fast and predictable performance with seamless scalability.

Dynamo DB features and benefits:

- NoSQL type of database (non-relational)
- Fast, highly available, and fully managed
- Used when data is fluid and can change

- Common use cases include social networks and web analytics

Push button scaling means that you can scale the DB at any time without incurring downtime.

SSD based and uses limited indexing on attributes for performance.

DynamoDB is a Web service that uses HTTP over SSL (HTTPS) as a transport and JSON as a message serialisation format.

Amazon DynamoDB stores three geographically distributed replicas of each table to enable high availability and data durability.

Data is synchronously replicated across 3 facilities (AZs) in a region.

Cross-region replication allows you to replicate across regions:

- Amazon DynamoDB global tables provides a fully managed solution for deploying a multi-region, multi-master database.

- When you create a global table, you specify the AWS regions where you want the table to be available.

- DynamoDB performs all of the necessary tasks to create identical tables in these regions and propagate ongoing data changes to all of them.

Provides low read and write latency.

Scale storage and throughput up or down as needed without code changes or downtime.

DynamoDB is schema-less.

DynamoDB can be used for storing session state.

Provides two read models:

1: Eventually consistent reads (Default):

- The eventual consistency option maximizes your read throughput (best read performance).

- An eventually consistent read might not reflect the results of a recently completed write.

- Consistency across all copies reached within 1 second.

2: Strongly consistent reads:

- A strongly consistent read returns a result that reflects all writes that received a successful response prior to the read (faster consistency).

Amazon DynamoDB Accelerator (DAX) is a fully managed, highly available, in-memory cache for DynamoDB that delivers up to a 10x performance improvement – from milliseconds to microseconds – even at millions of requests per second.

AMAZON REDSHIFT   SQL

Amazon Redshift is a fast, fully managed data warehouse that makes it simple and cost-effective to analyze all your data using standard SQL and existing Business Intelligence (BI) tools.

RedShift is a SQL based data warehouse **used for analytics applications**.

RedShift is a relational database that is used for Online Analytics Processing (OLAP) use cases.

RedShift is used for running complex analytic queries against petabytes of structured data, using sophisticated query optimization, columnar storage on high-performance local disks, and massively parallel query execution.

RedShift is ideal for **processing** large amounts of data for business intelligence.

RedShift is 10x faster than a traditional SQL DB.

RedShift uses columnar data storage:

- Data is stored sequentially in columns instead of rows.

- Columnar based DB is ideal for data warehousing and analytics.

- Requires fewer I/Os which greatly enhances performance.

RedShift provides advanced compression:

- Data is stored sequentially in columns which allows for much better performance and less storage space.

- RedShift automatically selects the compression scheme.

RedShift uses replication and continuous backups to enhance availability and improve durability and can automatically recover from component and node failures.

RedShift always keeps three copies of your data:

- The original

- A replica on compute nodes (within the cluster)

- A backup copy on S3

RedShift provides continuous/incremental backups:

- Multiple copies within a cluster

- Continuous and incremental backups to S3

- Continuous and incremental backups across regions

- Streaming restore

RedShift provides fault tolerance for the following failures:

- Disk failures

- Nodes failures

- Network failure

- AZ/region level disasters

AMAZON ELASTICACHE

ElastiCache is a web service that makes it easy to deploy and run Memcached or Redis protocol-compliant server nodes in the cloud.

The in-memory caching provided by ElastiCache can be used to significantly improve latency and throughput for many read-heavy application workloads or compute-intensive workloads.

Best for scenarios where the DB load is based on Online Analytics Processing (OLAP) transactions.

The following table describes a few **typical use cases for ElastiCache**:

Use Case	Benefit
Web session store	In cases with load-balanced web servers, store web session information in Redis so if a server is lost, the session info is not lost and another web server can pick it up
Database caching	Use Memcached in front of AWS RDS to cache popular queries to offload work from RDS and return results faster to users
Leaderboards	Use Redis to provide a live leaderboard for millions of users of your mobile app
Streaming data dashboards	Provide a landing spot for streaming sensor data on the factory floor, providing live real-time dashboard displays

Elasticache EC2 nodes cannot be accessed from the Internet, nor can they be accessed by EC2 instances in other VPCs.

Can be on-demand or reserved instances too (but not Spot instances).

Elasticache can be used for storing session state.

There are two types of ElastiCache engine:

- Memcached – simplest model, can run large nodes with multiple cores/threads, can be scaled in and out, can cache objects such as DBs.

- Redis – complex model, supports encryption, master / slave replication, cross AZ (HA), automatic failover and backup/restore.

The table below describes the requirements that would determine whether to use the Memcached or Redis engine:

Memcached	Redis
Simple, no-frills	You need encryption
You need to scale-out and in as demand changes	You need HIPAA compliance
You need to run multiple CPU cores and threads	Support for clustering
You need to cache objects (e.g. database queries)	You need complex data types
	You need HA (replication
	Pub/Sub capability
	Geospacial Indexing
	Backup and restore

AWS DATABASE QUIZ QUESTIONS

Answers and explanations are provided below after the last question in this section.

Question 1: Amazon Relational Database Service (RDS) is an example of what type of database?

A. Online transaction processing (OLTP)

B. Online analytics processing (OLAP)

C. No-SQL

D. Data warehouse

Question 2: Which AWS database service offers seamless horizontal scaling?

A. Amazon RDS *EC2*

B. Amazon RDS *EC2*   *EC2 — Vertical*

C. Amazon DynamoDB

D. Database on Amazon EC2

Question 3: How can fault tolerance be added to an Amazon RDS database?

A. Using read replicas

B. Using multi-AZ

C. Using Global Replicas

D. Using EBS snapshots

Question 4: How can an organization enable microsecond latency for a DynamoDB database?

A. Using Amazon ElastiCache

B. Using DynamoDB Auto Scaling

C. Using Read Replicas

D. Using DynamoDB Accelerator (DAX)

SQL

Question 5: Which AWS database service is a relational, data warehouse?

A. Amazon RedShift

B. Amazon RDS Aurora

C. Amazon DynamoDB

D. Amazon ElastiCache

Question 6: Why might an organization decide to move an on-premises database to Amazon RDS?

A. To reduce operational overhead *fully managed*

B. To increase flexibility

C. To eliminate the need to patch management

D. To benefit from seamless scalability

Question 7: How do you increase the capacity of an Amazon RDS database?

A. Scaling horizontally, by adding instances

B. Scaling horizontally, by adding RCUs/WCUs

C. Scaling vertically, by changing instance type

D. Scaling vertically by adding CPUs

Question 8: Amazon DynamoDB is good for which use case?

A. Structured data, rigid schema

B. Unstructured data, flexible schema   *No Sql - nor relational*

AWS DATABASE ANSWERS

Question 1, Answer: A

Explanation:

A is correct. Amazon RDS is an example of a relational database used for online transaction processing (OLTP) workloads. This means its typically used for production databases that process transactions.

B is incorrect. Amazon RDS is not well suited for OLAP workloads.

C is incorrect. Amazon RDS is a relational database, not a No-SQL type of database.

D is incorrect. Amazon RDS is not well suited to be a data warehouse. Amazon RedShift is a better option.

Question 2, Answer: C

Explanation:

A is incorrect. Amazon RDS runs on EC2 instances so you have to scale vertically by changing instance types.

B is incorrect. Amazon RedShift runs on EC2 instances so you have to scale vertically by changing instance types.

C is incorrect. Amazon DynamoDB offers seamless "push-button" horizontal scaling.

D is incorrect. If you run a 3rd party DB on EC2 instances so you have to scale vertically by changing instance types.

Question 3, Answer: B

Explanation:

A is incorrect. Read replicas are used for offloading database reads to improve performance.

B is correct. Multi-AZ creates a standby copy of the master DB in a separate availability zone.

C is incorrect. Global replicas are not a feature of Amazon RDS.

D is incorrect. Snapshots are used to take a point-in-time backup of the database, not for fault tolerance.

Question 4, Answer: D

Explanation:

A is incorrect. Amazon ElastiCache is not typically used in front of DynamoDB.

B is incorrect. This will allow the database to scale but will not achieve microsecond latency.

C is incorrect. Read replicas are used for offloading database reads to improve performance. These are associated with Amazon RDS, not DynamoDB.

D is correct. DynamoDB Accelerator (DAX) is an in-memory cache that increases performance of DynamoDB databases.

Question 5, Answer: A

Explanation:

A is correct. RedShift is a relational, SQL database that is well suited for data warehouse use.

B is incorrect. Amazon RDS Aurora is a relational database more suitable to transactional workloads rather than data warehouse workloads.

C is incorrect. Amazon DynamoDB is a No-SQL database used for transactional workloads.

D is incorrect. Amazon ElastiCache is an in-memory cache database.

Question 6, Answer: A

Explanation:

A is correct. You can reduce operational overhead by moving to AWS managed services. With RDS this means you no longer need to manage the operating system.

B is incorrect. You do not increase flexibility by moving to Amazon RDS. As it is a managed, hosted service, you will lose some flexibility.

C is incorrect. You do not eliminate the need for patch management on Amazon RDS. Updates are applied during maintenance windows.

D is incorrect. You do not get seamless scalability with RDS. To scale you need to change the instance type which incurs some downtime.

Question 7, Answer: C

Explanation:

A is incorrect. You do not scale Amazon RDS by adding instances, you must scale RDS vertically.

B is incorrect. You do not add RCUs/WCUs to Amazon RDS - these are used for scaling the capacity of an Amazon DynamoDB database.

C is correct. You can scale Amazon RDS by changing to a larger instance type. This is an example of vertical scaling.

D is incorrect. You need to change instance types to scale RDS, you cannot just add CPUs.

Question 8, Answer: B

Explanation:

A is incorrect. Structured data with a rigid schema is a description for a relational SQL type of database such as Amazon RDS.

B is correct. DynamoDB is a No-SQL database which has a flexible schema and is good for unstructured data.

ELASTIC LOAD BALANCING AND AUTO SCALING

AMAZON ELASTIC LOAD BALANCING (ELB)

ELB automatically distributes incoming application traffic across multiple targets, such as Amazon EC2 instances, containers, and IP addresses.

ELB can handle the varying load of your application traffic in a single Availability Zone or across multiple Availability Zones.

ELB features high availability, automatic scaling and robust security necessary to make your applications fault tolerant.

There are three types of Elastic Load Balancer (ELB) on AWS:

- **Application Load Balancer (ALB)** – layer 7 load balancer that routes connections based on the content of the request.

- **Network Load Balancer (NLB)** – layer 4 load balancer that routes connections based on IP protocol data.

- **Classic Load Balancer (CLB)** – this is the oldest of the three and provides basic load balancing at both layer 4 and layer 7.

APPLICATION LOAD BALANCER (ALB)

ALB is best suited for load balancing of HTTP and HTTPS traffic and provides advanced request routing targeted at the delivery of modern application architectures, including microservices and containers.

Operating at the individual request level (Layer 7), Application Load Balancer routes traffic to targets within Amazon Virtual Private Cloud (Amazon VPC) based on the content of the request.

NETWORK LOAD BALANCER (NLB)

NLB is best suited for load balancing of TCP traffic where extreme performance is required.

Operating at the connection level (Layer 4), Network Load Balancer routes traffic to targets within Amazon Virtual Private Cloud (Amazon VPC) and is capable of handling millions of requests per second while maintaining ultra-low latencies.

Network Load Balancer is also optimized to handle sudden and volatile traffic patterns.

CLASSIC LOAD BALANCER (CLB)

CLB provides basic load balancing across multiple Amazon EC2 instances and operates at both the request level and connection level.

Classic Load Balancer is intended for applications that were built within the EC2-Classic network.

The CLB may be phased out over time and Amazon are promoting the ALB and NLB for most use cases within VPC.

Benefits:

- ELB provides high availability and fault tolerance by allowing traffic to be directed to multiple EC2 instances.

AWS AUTO SCALING

AWS Auto Scaling automates the process of adding (scaling up) OR removing (scaling down) EC2 instances based on the traffic demand for your application.

Auto Scaling helps to ensure that you have the correct number of EC2 instances available to handle the application load.

You create collections of EC2 instances, called Auto Scaling Group (ASG).

You can specify the minimum number of instances in each ASG and AWS Auto Scaling will ensure the group never goes beneath this size.

You can also specify the maximum number of instances in each ASG and the group will never go above this size.

A desired capacity can be configured, and AWS Auto Scaling will ensure the group has this number of instances.

You can also specify scaling policies that control when Auto Scaling launches or terminates instances.

Scaling policies determine when, if and how the ASG scales and shrinks (on-demand/dynamic scaling, cyclic/scheduled scaling).

Scaling Plans define the triggers and when instances should be provisioned/de-provisioned.

A launch configuration is the template used to create new EC2 instances and includes parameters such as instance family, instance type, AMI, key pair and security groups.

Benefits:

- Auto Scaling enables elasticity and scalability

ELASTIC LOAD BALANCING AND AUTO SCALING QUIZ QUESTIONS

Answers and explanations are provided below after the last question in this section.

Question 1: How can a company enable elasticity for an application running on Amazon EC2?

A. By using Amazon EC2 Auto Scaling

B. By using Elastic Load Balancing

C. By configuring multi-AZ

D. By enabling failover in Amazon EC2

Question 2: Which type of Elastic Load Balancer can direct traffic based on the domain name?

A. Classic Load Balancer

B. Network Load Balancer

C. Application Load Balancer

D. Amazon EC2 Load Balancer

Question 3: How does Amazon EC2 Auto Scaling assist with cost-effectiveness?

A. By choosing the most cost-effective instance type

B. By balancing load between instances evenly

C. By launching and terminating instances as demand changes

D. By automating application failover

Question 4: How does Elastic Load Balancing (ELB) assist with fault tolerance?

A. By distributing connections to multiple back-end instances

B. By directing traffic according to latency

C. By caching content closer to users

D. By automatically launching instances

Question 5: Which of the following statements is INCORRECT about Elastic Load Balancing?

A. ELB can distribute connections across availability zones

B. ELB can be Internet facing

C. ELB enables high availability and fault tolerance

D. ELB can distribute connections across regions

Question 6: What does Elastic Load Balancing use to ensure instances are available?

A. EC2 Status Checks

B. CloudWatch Metrics

C. Scaling Plans

D. Health Checks

Question 7: Which type of Elastic Load Balancer routes connections based on IP protocol data at layer 4 only?

A. Classic Load Balancer

B. Network Load Balancer

C. Application Load Balancer

Question 8: What type of template is used by Amazon EC2 Auto Scaling to define instance family, AMI key pair, and security groups?

A. Scaling Plan

B. Launch Configuration

C. Scaling Policy

D. Auto Scaling Group

ELASTIC LOAD BALANCING AND AUTO SCALING ANSWERS

Question 1, Answer: A

Explanation:

A is correct. Amazon EC2 Auto Scaling enables elasticity for EC2 by launching and terminating instances as demand changes.

B is incorrect. Elastic Load Balancing is used for distributing connections to multiple instances but does not elastically scale the EC2 instances.

C is incorrect. This is not a setting you can configure for EC2.

D is incorrect. Failover may be something you can configure in your application, but it's not something you can configure in Amazon EC2.

Question 2, Answer: C

Explanation:

A is incorrect. The classic load balancer cannot do host-based routing.

B is incorrect. The network load balancer cannot do host-based routing.

C is correct. The application load balancer can do host-based routing which means it can direct traffic based on information in the host header such as a domain name.

D is incorrect. This is not a type of Amazon ELB.

Question 3, Answer: C

Explanation:

A is incorrect. Amazon EC2 Auto Scaling does not choose the most cost-effective instance type for you, you need to choose the instance type to use in the launch configuration.

B is incorrect. This is what Elastic Load Balancing does, and it's not a way of being more cost-effective, it's a way of being more fault-tolerant.

C is correct. Amazon EC2 Auto Scaling launches and terminates instances as demand for your application changes, this ensures you are only paying for instances that you need to service demand.

D is incorrect. Amazon EC2 Auto Scaling does not automate application failover.

Question 4, Answer: A

Explanation:

A is correct. ELB distributes connections to multiple back-end instances and this means your application is fault tolerant. You should couple this with Auto Scaling to ensure the right number of back-end instances are available.

B is incorrect. ELB does not direct traffic according to latency, and this more about performance than fault tolerance anyway.

C is incorrect. This is not something ELB does. This is more of a performance thing and something Content Delivery Network (CDN) service like Amazon CloudFront does.

D is incorrect. EC2 Auto Scaling is responsible for launching instances, not ELB.

Question 5, Answer: D

Explanation:

A is incorrect. ELB can handle the varying load of your application traffic in a single Availability Zone or across multiple Availability Zones.

B is incorrect. ELBs can be Internet-facing or internal .

C is incorrect. ELB enables high availability and fault tolerance.

D is correct. ELB cannot distribute connections across regions, only availability zones. To direct traffic across regions use Amazon Route 53.

Question 6, Answer: D

Explanation:

A is incorrect. EC2 Status Checks are used by Auto Scaling to check if instances are healthy, but not by ELB.

B is incorrect. ELB does not receive CloudWatch metrics to tell it if an instance is healthy.

C is incorrect. Scaling Plans are used by EC2 Auto Scaling to control how to scale.

D is correct. Health checks are used by ELB to check that an instance is available and healthy.

Question 7, Answer: B

Explanation:

A is incorrect. The CLB operates at layer 4 and layer 7.

B is correct. The NLB operates at layer 4 of the OSI model only, routing connections based on IP protocol data.

C is incorrect. An ALB operates at layer 7 of the OSI model only, routing connections based on the content of the request.

Question 8, Answer: B

Explanation:

A is incorrect. Scaling Plans define the triggers and when instances should be provisioned/de-provisioned.

B is correct. A launch configuration is the template used to create new EC2 instances and includes parameters such as instance family, instance type, AMI, key pair and security groups.

C is incorrect. Scaling policies determine when, if, and how the ASG scales and shrinks (on-demand/dynamic scaling, cyclic/scheduled scaling).

D is incorrect. Auto Scaling Group (ASG) are collections of EC2 instances.

CONTENT DELIVERY AND DNS SERVICES

AMAZON ROUTE 53 *— Domain Name Service*

Route 53 is the AWS Domain Name Service.

Route 53 performs three main functions:

- **Domain registration** – Route 53 allows you to register domain names.

- **Domain Name Service (DNS)** – Route 53 translates name to IP addresses using a global network of authoritative DNS servers.

- **Health checking** – Route 53 sends automated requests to your application to verify that it's reachable, available and functional.

You can use any combination of these functions.

Route 53 benefits:

 *Global*

- Domain registration

- DNS service

- Traffic Flow (send users to the best endpoint)

- Health checking

- DNS failover (automatically change domain endpoint if system fails)

- Integrates with ELB, S3, and CloudFront as endpoints

Routing policies determine how Route 53 DNS responds to queries.

The following table highlights the **key function of each type of routing policy**:

Policy	What it Does
Simple	Simple DNS response providing the IP address associated with a name
Failover	If primary is down (based on health checks), routes to secondary destination
Geolocation	Uses geographic location you're in (e.g. Europe) to route you to the closest region
Geoproximity	Routes you to the closest region within a geographic area
Latency	Directs you based on the lowest latency route to resources
Multivalue answer	Returns several IP addresses and functions as a basic load balancer
Weighted	Uses the relative weights assigned to resources to determine which to route to

AMAZON CLOUDFRONT

CloudFront is a content delivery network (CDN) that allows you to store (cache) your content at "edge locations" located around the world.

FRONT = EDGE = CACHE

This allows customers to access content more quickly and provides security against DDoS attacks.

CloudFront can be used for data, videos, applications, and APIs.

CloudFront benefits:

- Cache content at Edge Location for fast distribution to customers.

- Built-in Distributed Denial of Service (DDoS) attack protection.

- Integrates with many AWS services (S3, EC2, ELB, Route 53, Lambda).

Origins and Distributions:

- An origin is the origin of the files that the CDN will distribute.

- Origins can be either an S3 bucket, an EC2 instance, an Elastic Load Balancer or Route 53 – can also be external (non-AWS).

- To distribute content with CloudFront you need to create a distribution.

- There are two types of distribution: Web Distribution and RTMP Distribution.

CloudFront uses Edge Locations and Regional Edge Caches:

- An edge location is the location where content is cached (separate to AWS regions/AZs).

- Requests are automatically routed to the nearest edge location.

- Regional Edge Caches are located between origin web servers and global edge locations and have a larger cache.

- Regional Edge caches aim to get content closer to users.

The diagram below shows where Regional Edge Caches and Edge Locations are placed in relation to end users:

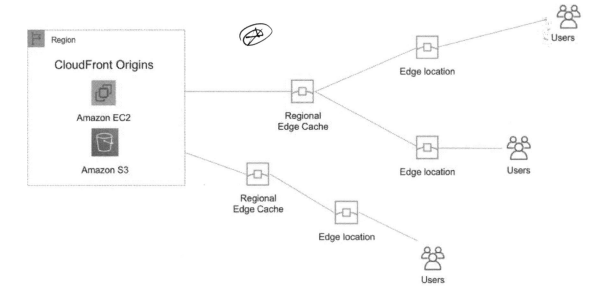

CONTENT DELIVERY AND DNS SERVICES QUIZ QUESTIONS

Answers and explanations are provided below after the last question in this section.

Question 1: How can an organization improve performance for users around the world accessing online videos?

A. Use Amazon Route 53 Failover routing

B. Create an Amazon CloudFront Distribution to host the videos   — *for caching*

C. Use Amazon S3 cross-region replication to distribute the media around the world

D. Use Amazon S3 Transfer acceleration to speed up downloads

Question 2: Which statement is NOT true about Amazon CloudFront Regional Edge Caches and Edge Locations?

A. A regional edge cache has a larger cache bandwidth than an edge location

B. There are more edge locations that regional edge caches

C. An edge location sits between a CloudFront Distribution and a regional edge cache

D. A regional edge cache sits between a CloudFront Distribution and an edge location

Question 3: What types of Origin does Amazon CloudFront support?

A. S3 bucket, EC2 instance

B. S3 bucket, RDS database

C. EC2 instance, EFS filesystem

D. EC2 instance, Auto Scaling Group

Question 4: Which services have a Global scope?

A. Amazon CloudFront, Amazon Route 53, Amazon VPC

B. Amazon CloudFront, Amazon Route 53, Amazon CloudWatch

C. AWS Lambda, Amazon CloudFront, Amazon Route 53

D. AWS IAM, Amazon CloudFront, Amazon Route 53
公共

Question 5: Which services does Amazon Route 53 provide?

A. Domain registration, DNS, firewall protection

B. Health checking, DNS, domain registration

C. Health checking, DNS, IP routing

D. Domain registration, DNS, content distribution

Question 6: Which service has built-in Distributed Denial of Service (DDoS) protection?

A. Amazon Route 53

B. Internet Gateway

C. Amazon CloudFront _shield_

D. AWS Direct Connect

Question 7: Which of the following is used to cache data to bring it closer to end users?

A. Amazon CloudFront Edge Location

B. Amazon CloudFront Distribution

C. Amazon CloudFront Origin

D. Amazon CloudFront Bucket

Question 8: In Amazon Route, what is the name for the configuration item that holds a collection of records belonging to a domain?

A. DNS record

B. Alias

C. Hosted zone

D. Routing Policy

- Edge Location - where content will be cached; read + write
- Origin - origin of all files that the CDN will distribute
- Distribution - name given to the CDN, consisting of a collection of Edge location
- Web distribution - for websites
- RTMP - for media streaming
- Cached => TTL: time to live (in seconds)

CONTENT DELIVERY AND DNS SERVICES ANSWERS

Question 1, Answer: B

Explanation:

A is incorrect. Amazon Route 53 failover routing policy is for failing between active / standby servers. This will not help in this scenario.

B is correct. Amazon CloudFront can be used to get the content cached around the world, closer to users, which will improve performance.

C is incorrect. This is not a good solution. This will get the content closer to users but you will now have lots of copies of data and need a method of directing traffic to each copy. This is operationally inefficient.

D is incorrect. Amazon S3 Transfer acceleration is used for improving uploads to S3, not downloads.

Question 2, Answer: C

Explanation:

A is incorrect. This is true, regional edge caches have a larger cache bandwidth than edge locations.

B is incorrect. There are more edge locations than regional edge locations.

C is correct. This statement is incorrect a regional edge cache sits between a CloudFront Distribution and an edge location.

D is incorrect. This statement is correct.

Question 3, Answer: A

Explanation:

A is correct. You can use S3 buckets and EC2 instances as origins for you CloudFront distribution. You can also use S3 static websites, other HTTP servers using Route 53, instances behind an ELB, and MediaStore Containers.

B is incorrect. You cannot configure an RDS database as an origin.

C is incorrect. You cannot configure an EFS filesystem as an origin.

D is incorrect. You cannot configure an ASG as an origin.

Question 4, Answer: D

Explanation:

A is incorrect. Amazon VPC has a regional scope.

B is incorrect. Amazon CloudWatch has a regional scope.

C is incorrect. AWS Lambda has a regional scope.

D is correct. All three of these services have a global scope.

Question 5, Answer: B

Explanation:

A is incorrect. Amazon Route 53 does not provide firewall protection.

B is correct. These are the core features of Amazon Route 53.

C is incorrect. Don't confuse routing here with the routing policies in Route 53. Amazon Route 53 is a DNS service that can "route" DNS requests, it does not do IP routing which is a network function.

D is incorrect. Amazon Route 53 does not provide content distribution (CloudFront does).

Question 6, Answer: C

Explanation:

A is incorrect. Amazon Route 53 does not have DDoS protection features.

B is incorrect. An Internet Gateway does not have DDoS protection features.

C is correct. Amazon CloudFront has built-in Distributed Denial of Service (DDoS) attack protection.

D is incorrect. AWS Direct Connect does not have DDoS protection features.

Question 7, Answer: A

Explanation:

A is correct. Edge Locations are part of the AWS Global Infrastructure and are located around the world. They are used to cache content to bring it closer to end users for improved performance.

B is incorrect. A distribution is created within Amazon CloudFront. This is how you configure your origin, settings, and where to cache your file. It is not where the files are cached.

C is incorrect. An origin is the source of the media that needs to be cached around the world.

D is incorrect. A bucket is an Amazon S3 container for holding objects. An S3 bucket can be an origin but it is not where data is cached, it is where it is sourced from.

Question 8, Answer: C

Explanation:

A is incorrect. A DNS record is an individual record, not a collection of records.

B is incorrect. An Alias is a type of record that points to an AWS resource.

C is correct. A hosted zone represents a set of records belonging to a domain.

D is incorrect. A routing policy determines how Route 53 responds to a query (what records it returns).

MONITORING AND LOGGING SERVICES

AMAZON CLOUDWATCH

- Personal Trainer

Amazon CloudWatch is a monitoring service for AWS cloud resources and the applications you run on AWS.

CloudWatch is for performance monitoring (CloudTrail is for auditing).

Used to collect and track metrics, collect and monitor log files, and set alarms.

Automatically react to changes in your AWS resources.

Monitor resources such as:

- EC2 instances
- DynamoDB tables
- RDS DB instance
- Custom metrics generated by applications and services
- Any log files generated by your applications

Gain system-wide visibility into resource utilization.

CloudWatch monitoring includes application performance.

Monitor operational health.

CloudWatch is accessed via API, command-line interface, AWS SDKs, and the AWS Management Console.

CloudWatch integrates with IAM.

Amazon CloudWatch Logs lets you monitor and troubleshoot your systems and applications using your existing system, application and custom log files.

CloudWatch Logs can be used for real time application and system monitoring as well as long term log retention.

CloudWatch Logs keeps logs indefinitely by default.

CloudTrail logs can be sent to CloudWatch Logs for real-time monitoring.

CloudWatch Logs metric filters can evaluate CloudTrail logs for specific terms, phrases or values.

CloudWatch retains metric data as follows:

- Data points with a period of less than 60 seconds are available for 3 hours. These data points are high-resolution custom metrics.
- Data points with a period of 60 seconds (1 minute) are available for 15 days.
- Data points with a period of 300 seconds (5 minute) are available for 63 days.
- Data points with a period of 3600 seconds (1 hour) are available for 455 days (15 months).

Dashboards allow you to create, customize, interact with, and save graphs of AWS resources and custom metrics.

Alarms can be used to monitor any Amazon CloudWatch metric in your account.

Events are a stream of system events describing changes in your AWS resources.

Logs help you to aggregate, monitor and store logs.

Basic monitoring = 5 mins (free for EC2 Instances, EBS volumes, ELBs and RDS DBs).

Detailed monitoring = 1 min (chargeable).

Metrics are provided automatically for a number of AWS products and services.

There is no standard metric for memory usage on EC2 instances.

A custom metric is any metric you provide to Amazon CloudWatch (e.g., time to load a web page or application performance).

Options for storing logs:

- CloudWatch Logs
- Centralized logging system (e.g., Splunk)
- Custom script and store on S3

Do not store logs on non-persistent disks:

Best practice is to store logs in CloudWatch Logs or S3.

CloudWatch Logs subscription can be used across multiple AWS accounts (using cross account access).

Amazon CloudWatch uses Amazon SNS to send email.

AWS CLOUDTRAIL

AWS CloudTrail is a web service that records activity made on your account and delivers log files to an Amazon S3 bucket.

CloudTrail is for auditing (CloudWatch is for performance monitoring).

CloudTrail is about logging and saves a history of API calls for your AWS account.

Provides visibility into user activity by recording actions taken on your account.

API history enables security analysis, resource change tracking, and compliance auditing.

Logs API calls made via:

- AWS Management Console
- AWS SDKs
- Command line tools
- Higher-level AWS services (such as CloudFormation)

CloudTrail records account activity and service events from most AWS services and logs the following records:

- The identity of the API caller
- The time of the API call
- The source IP address of the API caller

- The request parameters

- The response elements returned by the AWS service

CloudTrail is not enabled by default.

CloudTrail is per AWS account.

You can consolidate logs from multiple accounts using an S3 bucket:

- Turn on CloudTrail in the paying account.

- Create a bucket policy that allows cross-account access.

- Turn on CloudTrail in the other accounts and use the bucket in the paying account.

You can integrate CloudTrail with CloudWatch Logs to deliver data events captured by CloudTrail to a CloudWatch Logs log stream.

CloudTrail log file integrity validation feature allows you to determine whether a CloudTrail log file was unchanged, deleted, or modified since CloudTrail delivered it to the specified Amazon S3 bucket.

MONITORING AND LOGGING SERVICES QUIZ QUESTIONS

Answers and explanations are provided below after the last question in this section.

Question 1: Which service can be used for alerting if the CPU is heavily loaded on an EC2 instance?

A. Amazon CloudWatch   *performance*

B. Amazon CloudTrail

Question 2: Which statement about Amazon CloudWatch is INCORRECT?

A. CloudWatch Logs collects and centralizes logs from AWS resources

B. CloudWatch Alarms can be set to react to changes in your resources

C. CloudWatch monitoring can include application performance

D. CloudWatch only integrates with Amazon EC2

Question 3: Which service can be used to record information about API activity in your AWS account?

A. Amazon CloudWatch

B. Amazon CloudTrail

Question 4: Does Amazon CloudTrail permanently record all API activity in your account by default?

A. Yes   *persistent*

B. No

MONITORING AND LOGGING SERVICES ANSWERS

Question 1, Answer: A

Explanation:

A is correct. CloudWatch is used for performance monitoring.

B is incorrect. CloudTrail is used for auditing, not performance monitoring.

Question 2, Answer: D

Explanation:

A is incorrect. This statement is correct.

B is incorrect. This statement is correct.

C is incorrect. This statement is correct.

D is correct. This is not true, CloudWatch integrates with most AWS services.

Question 3, Answer: B

Explanation:

A is incorrect. CloudWatch is used for performance monitoring, not auditing of API activity.

B is correct. This is correct. CloudTrail can keep a record of all API activity in your account.

Question 4, Answer: B

Explanation:

A is incorrect.

B is correct. This is a true statement, by default Amazon CloudTrail only keeps 90 days of records. To keep records permanently you need to create a Trail and record events to an Amazon S3 bucket.

NOTIFICATION SERVICES

AMAZON SIMPLE NOTIFICATION SERVICE (SNS)

Amazon Simple Notification Service (Amazon SNS) is a web service that makes it easy to set up, operate, and send notifications from the cloud.

Amazon SNS is used for building and integrating loosely-coupled, distributed applications.

SNS provides instantaneous, push-based delivery (no polling).

SNS concepts:

- **Topics** – how you label and group different endpoints that you send messages to.
- **Subscriptions** – the endpoints that a topic sends messages to.
- **Publishers** – the person/alarm/event that gives SNS the message that needs to be sent.

SNS usage:

- Send automated or manual notifications.
- Send notification to email, mobile (SMS), SQS, and HTTP endpoints.
- Closely integrated with other AWS services such as CloudWatch so that alarms, events, and actions in your AWS account can trigger notifications.

Uses simple APIs and easy integration with applications.

Flexible message delivery is provided over multiple transport protocols.

Offered under an inexpensive, pay-as-you-go model with no up-front costs.

The web-based AWS Management Console offers the simplicity of a point-and-click interface.

Data type is JSON.

SNS supports a wide variety of needs including event notification, monitoring applications, workflow systems, time-sensitive information updates, mobile applications, and any other application that generates or consumes notifications.

SNS Subscribers:

- HTTP
- HTTPS
- Email
- Email-JSON
- SQS
- Application
- Lambda

SNS supports notifications over multiple transport protocols:

- **HTTP/HTTPS** – subscribers specify a URL as part of the subscription registration.

- **Email/Email-JSON** – messages are sent to registered addresses as email (text-based or JSON-object).
- **SQS** – users can specify an SQS standard queue as the endpoint.
- **SMS** – messages are sent to registered phone numbers as SMS text messages.

Topic names are limited to 256 characters.

SNS supports CloudTrail auditing for authenticated calls.

SNS provides durable storage of all messages that it receives (across multiple AZs).

BILLING AND PRICING

GENERAL PRICING INFORMATION

AWS Billing and Pricing is one of the key subjects on the Cloud Practitioner exam. It is recommended to read the following whitepaper to understand how AWS pricing works: https://d1.awsstatic.com/whitepapers/aws_pricing_overview.pdf.

AWS works on a pay as you go model in which you only pay for what you use, when you are using it.

If you turn off resources, you don't pay for them (you may pay for consumed storage).

There are no upfront charges and you stop paying for a service when you stop using it.

Aside from EC2 reserved instances you are not locked into long term contracts and can terminate whenever you choose to.

Volume discounts are available so the more you use a service the cheaper it gets (per unit used).

There are no termination fees.

The three fundamental drivers of cost with AWS are: compute, storage and outbound data transfer.

In most cases, there is no charge for inbound data transfer or for data transfer between other AWS services within the same region (there are some exceptions).

Outbound data transfer is aggregated across services and then charged at the outbound data transfer rate.

Free tier allows you to run certain resources for free.

Free tier includes offers that expire after 12 months and offers that never expire.

Pricing policies include:

- Pay as you go
- Pay less when you reserve
- Pay even less per unit when using more
- Pay even less as AWS grows
- Custom pricing (enterprise customers only)

Free services include:

- Amazon VPC
- Elastic Beanstalk (but not the resources created)
- CloudFormation (but not the resources created)
- Identity Access Management (IAM)
- Auto Scaling (but not the resources created)
- OpsWorks
- Consolidated Billing

Fundamentally charges include:

- Compute
- Storage
- Data out

AMAZON EC2 PRICING

EC2 pricing is based on:

- Clock hours of server uptime — *Second or hour*
- Instance configuration
- Instance type
- Number of instances
- Load balancing
- Detailed monitoring
- Auto Scaling (resources created)
- Elastic IP addresses (charged if allocated but not used)
- Operating systems and software packages

There are several pricing models for AWS services, these include:

On Demand: *Pay as you go , short. spiky , non-interrupted*

- Means you pay for compute or database capacity with no long-term commitments of upfront payments.
- You pay for the computer capacity per hour or per second (Linux only, and applies to On-Demand, Reserved and Spot instances).
- Recommended for users who prefer low cost and flexibility without upfront payment or long-term commitments.
- Good for applications with short-term, spiky, or unpredictable workloads that cannot be interrupted.

Dedicated Hosts:

- A dedicated host is an EC2 servers dedicated to a single customer.
- Runs in your VPC.
- Good for when you want to leverage existing server-bound software licences such as Windows Server, SQL Server, and SUSE Linux Enterprise Server.
- Also good for meeting compliance requirements.

Dedicated Instances:

- Dedicated Instances are Amazon EC2 instances that run in a VPC on hardware that is dedicated to a single customer.
- Dedicated instances are physically isolated at the host hardware level from instances that belong to other AWS accounts.

- Dedicated instances may share hardware with other instances from the same AWS account that are not Dedicated instances.

Spot Instances: *flexible*

- Purchase spare computing capacity with no upfront commitment at discounted hourly rates.
- Provides up to 90% off the On-Demand price.
- Recommended for applications that have flexible start and end times, applications that are only feasible at very low compute prices, and users with urgent computing needs for a lot of additional capacity.
- In the old model Spot instances were terminated because of higher competing bids, in the new model this does not happen, but instances still may be terminated (with a 2-minute warning) when EC2 needs the capacity back – note: the exam may not be updated to reflect this yet.

Reservations: *predictable*

- Reserved instances provide significant discounts, up to 75% compared to On-Demand pricing, by paying for capacity ahead of time.
- Provide a capacity reservation when applied to a specific Availability Zone.
- Good for applications that have predictable usage, that need reserved capacity, and for customers who can commit to a 1 or 3-year term.

Reservations apply to various services, including:

- Amazon EC2 Reserved Instances
- Amazon DynamoDB Reserved Capacity
- Amazon ElastiCache Reserved Nodes
- Amazon RDS Reserved Instances
- Amazon RedShift Reserved Instances

Reservation options include no upfront, partial upfront and all upfront.
Reservation terms are 1 or 3 years.

AMAZON SIMPLE STORAGE SERVICE (S3) PRICING

Storage pricing is determined by:

- **Storage class** – e.g. Standard or IA
- **Storage quantity** – data volume stored in your buckets on a per GB basis
- **Number of requests** – the number and type of requests, e.g. GET, PUT, POST, LIST, COPY
- **Lifecycle transitions requests** – moving data between storage classes
- **Data transfer** – data transferred out of an S3 region is charged

AMAZON GLACIER PRICING

- Extremely low cost and you pay only for what you need with no commitments of upfront fees.

- Charged for requests and data transferred out of Glacier.

- "Amazon Glacier Select" pricing allows queries to run directly on data stored on Glacier without having to retrieve the archive. Priced on amount of data scanned, returned, and number of requests initiated.

- **Three options for access to archives**, listed in the table below:

	Expedited	Standard	Bulk
Data access time	1-5 minutes	3-5 hours	5-12 hours
Data retrievals	$0.03 per GB	$0.01 per GB	$0.0025 per GB
Retrieval requests	On-Demand: $0.01 per request Provisioned: $100 per Provisioned Capacity Unit	$0.050 per 1,000 requests	$0.025 per 1,000 requests

AWS SNOWBALL PRICING

Pay a service fee per data transfer job and the cost of shipping the appliance.

Each job allows use of Snowball appliance for 10 days onsite for free.

Data transfer into AWS is free and outbound is charged (per region pricing).

AMAZON RELATIONAL DATABASE SERVICE (RDS) PRICING

RDS pricing is determined by:

- **Clock hours of server uptime** – amount of time the DB instance is running

- **Database characteristics** – e.g. database engine, size and memory class

- **Database purchase type** – e.g. On-Demand, Reserved

- **Number of database instances**

- **Provisioned storage** – backup is included up to 100% of the size of the DB. After the DB is terminated backup storage is charged per GB per month

- **Additional storage** – the amount of storage in addition to the provisioned storage is charged per GB per month

- **Requests** – the number of input and output requests to the DB

- **Deployment type** – single AZ or multi-AZ

- **Data transfer** – inbound is free, outbound data transfer costs are tiered

- **Reserved Instances** – RDS RIs can be purchased with No Upfront, Partial Upfront, or All Upfront terms. Available for Aurora, MySQL, MariaDB, Oracle and SQL Server

AMAZON CLOUDFRONT PRICING

CloudFront pricing is determined by:

- **Traffic distribution** – data transfer and request pricing, varies across regions, and is based on the edge location from which the content is served.

- **Requests** – the number and type of requests (HTTP or HTTPS) and the geographic region in which they are made.

- **Data transfer out** – quantity of data transferred out of CloudFront edge locations.

- There are additional chargeable items such as invalidation requests, field-level encryption requests, and custom SSL certificates.

AWS LAMBDA PRICING

Pay only for what you use and charged based on the number of requests for functions and the time it takes to execute the code.

Price is dependent on the amount of memory allocated to the function.

AMAZON ELASTIC BLOCK STORE (EBS) PRICING

Pricing is based on three factors:

- **Volumes** – volume storage for all EBS volumes type is charged by the amount of GB provisioned per month.

- **Snapshots** – based on the amount of space consumed by snapshots in S3. Copying snapshots is charged on the amount of data copied across regions.

- **Data transfer** – inbound data transfer is free, outbound data transfer charges are tiered.

AMAZON DYNAMODB PRICING

Charged based on:

- Provisioned throughput (write)

- Provisioned throughput (read)

- Indexed data storage

- **Data transfer** – no charge for data transfer between DynamoDB and other AWS services within the same region, across regions is charged on both sides of the transfer.

- **Global tables** – charged based on the resources associated with each replica of the table (replicated write capacity units, or rWCUs).

- **Reserved Capacity** – option available for a one-time upfront fee and commitment to paying a minimum usage level at specific hourly rates for the duration of the term. Additional throughput is charged at standard rates.

The table below provides more details:

Resource Type	Details	Monthly Price
Provisioned throughput (write)	One write capacity unit (WCU) provides up to one write per second, enough for 2.5 million writes per month	As low as $0.47 per WCU
Provisioned throughput (read)	One read capacity unit (RCU) provides up to two reads per second, enough for 5.2 million reads per month	As low as $0.09 per RCU
Indexed data storage	DynamoDB charges an hourly rate per GB of disk space that your table consumes	As low as $0.25 per GB

Always remember that AWS is fundamentally a service in which you pay only for what you use and can start and stop using services whenever you choose.

You do not have to enter into any contracts however you may choose to do so for lower pricing.

AWS SUPPORT PLANS

There are **four AWS support plans** available:

- **Basic** – billing and account support only (access to forums only) $0 /mo
- **Developer** – business hours support via email $29/mo
- **Business** – 24×7 email, chat and phone support $100/mo
- **Enterprise** – 24×7 email, chat and phone support $15 k/mo

Enterprise support comes with a Technical Account Manager (TAM).

Developer allows one person to open unlimited cases.

Business and Enterprise allow unlimited contacts to open unlimited cases.

The table below highlights the **features of each support plan** (make sure you know these for the exam):

	Basic	Developer	Business	Enterprise
Customer Service and Communities	24x7 access to customer service, documentation, whitepapers, and support forums	24x7 access to customer service, documentation, whitepapers, and support forums	24x7 access to customer service, documentation, whitepapers, and support forums	24x7 access to customer service, documentation, whitepapers, and support forums
Best Practices	Access to 7 core Trusted Advisor checks	Access to 7 core Trusted Advisor checks	Access to full set of Trusted Advisor checks	Access to full set of Trusted Advisor checks
Health status and Notifications	Access to Personal Health Dashboard	Access to Personal Health Dashboard	Access to Personal Health Dashboard & Health API	Access to Personal Health Dashboard & Health API
Technical Support		Business hours** access to Cloud Support Associates via email	24x7 access to Cloud Support Engineers via email, chat & phone	24x7 access to Sr. Cloud Support Engineers via email, chat & phone
Who Can Open Cases		One primary contact/ Unlimited cases	Unlimited contacts/ Unlimited cases (IAM supported)	Unlimited contacts/ Unlimited cases (IAM supported)
Case Severity/ Response Times*		General guidance: < 24 business hours System impaired: < 12 business hours	General guidance: < 24 hours System impaired: < 12 hours Production system impaired: < 4 hours Production system down: < 1 hour	General guidance: < 24 hours System impaired: < 12 hours Production system impaired: < 4 hours Production system down: < 1 hour Business-critical system down: < 15 minutes

RESOURCE GROUPS AND TAGGING

Tags are key / value pairs that can be attached to AWS resources.

Tags contain metadata (data about data).

Tags can sometimes be inherited – e.g. resources created by Auto Scaling, CloudFormation or Elastic Beanstalk.

Resource groups make it easy to group resources using the tags that are assigned to them. You can group resources that share one or more tags.

Resource groups contain general information, such as:

- Region
- Name
- Health Checks

Resource groups also contain specific information, such as:

- Public & private IP addresses (for EC2)
- Port configurations (for ELB)
- Database engine (for RDS)

AWS ORGANIZATIONS AND CONSOLIDATED BILLING

AWS organizations allows you to consolidate multiple AWS accounts into an organization that you create and centrally manage.

Available in two feature sets:

- Consolidated Billing
- All features

Includes root accounts and organizational units.

Policies are applied to root accounts or OUs.

Consolidated billing includes:

- **Paying Account** – independent and cannot access resources of other accounts.
- **Linked Accounts** – all linked accounts are independent.

Consolidated billing has the following **benefits**:

- **One bill** – You get one bill for multiple accounts.
- **Easy tracking** – You can track the charges across multiple accounts and download the combined cost and usage data.
- **Combined usage** – You can combine the usage across all accounts in the organization to share the volume pricing discounts and Reserved Instance discounts. This can result in a lower charge for your project, department, or company than with individual standalone accounts.
- **No extra fee** – Consolidated billing is offered at no additional cost.

Limit of 20 linked accounts (by default).

One bill for multiple AWS accounts.

Easy to track charges and allocate costs.

Volume pricing discounts can be applied to resources.

Billing alerts enabled on the Paying account include data for all Linked accounts (or can be created per Linked account).

Consolidated billing allows you to get volume discounts on all of your accounts.

Unused reserved instances (RIs) for EC2 are applied across the group.

CloudTrail is on a per account basis and per region basis but can be aggregated into a single bucket in the paying account.

Best practices:

- Always enable multi-factor authentication (MFA) on the root account.
- Always use a strong and complex password on the root account.
- The Paying account should be used for billing purposes only. Do not deploy resources into the Paying account.

AWS QUICK STARTS

Quick Starts are built by AWS solutions architects and partners to help you deploy popular solutions on AWS, based on AWS best practices for security and high availability.

These reference deployments implement key technologies automatically on the AWS Cloud, often with a single click and in less than an hour.

Leverages CloudFormation.

Budgets – before
Cost Explorer – after

AWS COST CALCULATORS AND TOOLS

- **AWS Cost Explorer** – enables you to visualize your usage patterns over time and to identify your underlying cost drivers. *After usage*
- **AWS Simple Monthly calculator** – shows you how much you would pay in AWS if you move your resources. *For biz cases → Before*

(Exam)

- **Total Cost of Ownership (TCO) calculator** – use to compare the cost of running your applications in an on-premise or colocation environment against AWS.

AWS COST EXPLORER   *13 + 3*

The AWS Cost Explorer is a free tool that allows you to view charts of your costs.

You can view cost data for the past 13 months and forecast how much you are likely to spend over the next three months.   *13 + 3*

Cost Explorer can be used to discover patterns in how much you spend on AWS resources over time and to identify cost problem areas.

Cost Explorer can help you **to identify service usage statistics** such as:

- Which services you use the most.
- View metrics for which AZ has the most traffic.
- Which linked account is used the most.

AWS SIMPLE MONTHLY CALCULATOR   — Budgets (before)

The AWS Simple Monthly Calculator helps customers and prospects estimate their monthly AWS bill more efficiently.

With the AWS Simple Monthly Calculator, you can add services in different regions.

The calculator includes support for most AWS services, and you can include additional costs such as data ingress/egress charges, data storage charges, and retrieval fees.

It is possible to select EC2 dedicated hosts and reserved instances with various pricing models.

Support can also be added.

TCO CALCULATOR

The TCO calculator is a free tool provided by AWS that allows you to estimate the cost savings of using the AWS Cloud vs. using an on-premised data center.

The TCO calculator therefore helps you to reduce Total Cost of Ownership (TCO) by avoiding large capital expenditures on hardware and infrastructure.

The TCO calculator can also provide directional guidance on cost savings.

The TCO calculator works by you inputting cost elements of your current/or estimated on-premises data center and comparing those cost requirements with how much it would cost on AWS.

Elements can be added/modified as you move through the process to best estimate the cost savings.

for biz cases
and presentations

BILLING AND PRICING QUIZ QUESTIONS

Answers and explanations are provided below after the last question in this section.

Question 1: Which pricing model is best suited for a batch computing workload that requires significant compute power and can be stopped at any time?

A. On-demand instances

B. Dedicated instances

C. Spot instances

D. Reserved instances

Question 2: Which AWS services are free?

A. Amazon EC2 Auto Scaling, CloudFormation, IAM

B. Amazon EC2, CloudFormation, IAM

C. Consolidated billing, EC2 Auto Scaling, NAT Gateway

D. IAM, Amazon S3, outbound data transfer

Question 3: With Amazon S3, which of the following are NOT chargeable items?

A. Quantity of data in S3 buckets

B. Lifecycle transitions

C. Transfer Acceleration

D. Inbound data transfer

Question 4: What is the most cost-effective storage tier for data that is not often accessed, will be retained for 7 years, and needs to be retrievable within 24 hours?

A. Amazon S3 Standard

B. Amazon S3 Glacier

C. Amazon S3 Standard-Infrequent Access

D. Amazon S3 Glacier Deep Archive

Question 5: What is a key cost advantage of moving to the AWS Cloud?

A. Many services are free

B. You can provision what you need and scale on demand

C. You can deploy services using an API

D. You can scale almost limitlessly

Question 6: Which storage classes are available for the Amazon Elastic File System?

A. Standard, Provisioned Throughput

B. Standard, Deep Archive

C. Standard, Infrequent Access Storage

D. Standard, One-Zone IA

Question 7: With Amazon Virtual Private Cloud (VPC) what must you pay for?

A. Internet Gateway

B. Route Table

C. Security Group

D. VPN Connection

Question 8: What can you use to assign metadata to AWS resources for cost reporting?

A. Labels

B. Tags

C. ARNs

D. Templates

Question 9: Which AWS pricing feature can be used to take advantage of volume pricing discounts across multiple accounts?

A. Consolidated billing

B. TCO Calculator

C. Enterprise Agreement

D. Cost Explorer

Question 10: What is the best tool for an organization to compare the cost of running on-premises to using the AWS Cloud?

A. Cost Explorer

B. Simple Monthly Calculator

C. TCO Calculator

D. Trusted Advisor

Question 11: Which AWS support plan comes with a Technical Account Manager (TAM)

A. Basic

B. Developer

C. Business

D. Enterprise

Question 12: Which of the following needs to be considered in a Total Cost of Ownership (TCO) analysis?

A. Data center operations costs

B. Application licensing costs

C. Company marketing campaign costs

Question 13: Which of the following is NOT a payment option for Amazon EC2 reserved instances?

A. No upfront

B. All upfront

C. All at the end

D. Partial upfront

Question 14: Which tool can an IT manager use to forecast costs over the next 3 months?

A. AWS Organizations

B. AWS TCO Calculator

C. AWS Cost Explorer $13+3$

D. Amazon CloudWatch

BILLING AND PRICING ANSWERS

Question 1, Answer: C

Explanation:

A is incorrect. On-demand would be very expensive for this type of workload.

B is incorrect. Dedicated instances are used when you need to run workloads on hardware that's dedicated to a single customer.

C is correct. Spot instances are great for this type of workload. You can achieve significant discounts which will mean a big cost saving for such a compute intensive workload. You can be stopped at any time if AWS need the capacity back but that's OK for some batch workloads.

D is incorrect. Reserved instances are better for stable long-running workloads where you can commit to a 1- or 3-year term.

Question 2, Answer: A

Explanation:

A is correct. All of these services are free of charge. However you do pay for resources created by Auto Scaling and CloudFormation.

B is incorrect. Amazon EC2 is not free of charge.

C is incorrect. NAT Gateways are not free of charge.

D is incorrect. Amazon S3 is not free of charge.

Question 3, Answer: D

Explanation:

A is incorrect. This is a chargeable item in Amazon S3.

B is incorrect. This is a chargeable item in Amazon S3.

C is incorrect. This is a chargeable item in Amazon S3.

D is correct. You do not pay for inbound data transfer, only outbound data transfer.

Question 4, Answer: D

Explanation:

A is incorrect. This is not the most affordable option for long term data storage.

B is incorrect. This is not the most affordable option for long term data storage where retrieval times of 24 hours are acceptable.

C is incorrect. This is not the most affordable option for long term data storage where retrieval times of 24 hours are acceptable.

D is correct. This is the most affordable option for long term data storage where retrieval times of 24 hours are acceptable.

Question 5, Answer: B

Explanation:

A is incorrect. This is true, but it's not the best reason to move to AWS as you still have to pay for most compute and storage services.

B is correct. This is a great reason to move to the cloud and a key cost benefit. This means you are only ever paying for resources that you are actually using, with little or no idle capacity.

C is incorrect. This is an advantage of the cloud, but not related to cost.

D is incorrect. This is true but not a key cost advantage.

Question 6, Answer: C

Explanation:

A is incorrect. Provisioned throughput is not a storage class, it is a way you can get better performance for additional cost.

B is incorrect. Deep Archive is a tier of Glacier storage, not EFS.

C is correct. These are the two storage classes available for EFS.

D is incorrect. One-Zone IA is an Amazon S3 storage class.

Question 7, Answer: D

Explanation:

A is incorrect. You do not need to pay for Internet Gateways.

B is incorrect. You do not need to pay for Route Tables.

C is incorrect. You do not need to pay for Security Groups.

D is correct. You need to pay for VPN Connection.

Question 8, Answer: B

Explanation:

A is incorrect. Labels are not used for assigning metadata to AWS resources.

B is correct. Tags and resource groups are great tools for assigning metadata to AWS resources and then being able to group resources that share one or more tags.

C is incorrect. ARNs are Amazon Resource Names and are not used for assigning metadata to AWS resources.

D is incorrect. Templates are not used for assigning metadata to AWS resources.

Question 9, Answer: A

Explanation:

A is correct. With Consolidated billing you can combine the usage across all accounts in the organization to share the volume pricing discounts and Reserved Instance discounts. This can result in a lower charge for your project, department, or company than with individual standalone accounts.

B is incorrect. The TCO calculator is a free tool provided by AWS that allows you to estimate the cost savings of using the AWS Cloud vs. using an on-premise data center.

C is incorrect. This is not an AWS pricing feature.

D is incorrect. The AWS Cost Explorer is a free tool that allows you to view charts of your costs. It is not used for taking advantage of volume pricing discounts across accounts.

Question 10, Answer: C

Explanation:

A is incorrect. Cost explorer is used for viewing and reporting on cost.

B is incorrect. In this case we want to perform a Total Cost of Ownership (TCO) analysis and this is not the best tool.

C is correct. The TCO calculator is a free tool provided by AWS that allows you to estimate the cost savings of using the AWS Cloud vs. using an on-premise data center.

D is incorrect. AWS Trusted Advisor is an online tool that provides you real time guidance to help you provision your resources following AWS best practices.

Question 11, Answer: D

Explanation:

A is incorrect. The basic plan does not come with a TAM.

B is incorrect. The developer plan does not come with a TAM.

C is incorrect. The business plan does not come with a TAM.

D is correct. Only the enterprise support plan comes with a TAM.

Question 12, Answer: A

Explanation:

A is correct. You need to include all costs that are being incurred to run on-premises so you can compare costs to the AWS cloud.

B is incorrect. You still need your application licenses in the cloud.

C is incorrect. This is not related to running your IT infrastructure on-premises so should not be included.

Question 13, Answer: C

Explanation:

A is incorrect. This is a payment option for Amazon EC2 reserved instances.

B is incorrect. This is a payment option for Amazon EC2 reserved instances.

C is correct. This is not a payment option for Amazon EC2 reserved instances.

D is incorrect. This is a payment option for Amazon EC2 reserved instances.

Question 14, Answer: C

Explanation:

A is incorrect. AWS organizations allows you to consolidate multiple AWS accounts into an organization that you create and centrally manage.

B is incorrect. The TCO calculator is a free tool provided by AWS that allows you to estimate the cost savings of using the AWS Cloud vs. using an on-premise data center.

C is correct. The AWS Cost Explorer is a free tool that allows you to view charts of your costs. You can view cost data for the past 13 months and forecast how much you are likely to spend over the next three months.

D is incorrect. Amazon CloudWatch is a monitoring tool and cannot be used for forecast future costs.

CLOUD SECURITY

GENERAL

As an AWS customer, you inherit all the best practices of AWS policies, architecture, and operational processes.

The AWS Cloud enables a shared responsibility model.

AWS manages security OF the cloud, you are responsible for security IN the cloud.

You retain control of the security you choose to implement to protect your own content, platform, applications, systems, and networks no differently than you would in an on-site data center.

BENEFITS OF AWS SECURITY

- **Keep Your Data Safe** – the AWS infrastructure puts strong safeguards in place to help.
- **Protect your privacy** – All data is stored in highly secure AWS data centers.
- **Meet Compliance Requirements** – AWS manages dozens of compliance programs in its infrastructure. This means that segments of your compliance have already been completed.
- **Save Money** – cut costs by using AWS data centers. Maintain the highest standard of s security without having to manage your own facility.
- **Scale Quickly** – security scales with your AWS Cloud usage. No matter the size of your business, the AWS infrastructure is designed to keep your data safe.

COMPLIANCE

AWS Cloud Compliance enables you to understand the robust controls in place at AWS to maintain security and data protection in the cloud.

As systems are built on top of AWS Cloud infrastructure, compliance responsibilities will be shared.

Compliance programs include:

- Certifications / attestations
- Laws, regulations, and privacy
- Alignments / frameworks

AWS CONFIG

AWS Config is a fully-managed service that provides you with an AWS resource inventory, configuration history, and configuration change notifications to enable security and regulatory compliance.

With AWS Config, you can discover existing and deleted AWS resources, determine your overall compliance against rules, and dive into configuration details of a resource at any point in time. AWS Config enables compliance auditing, security analysis, resource change tracking, and troubleshooting.

AWS SERVICE CATALOG   *customized*   *in-house approval*

You can use AWS Service Catalog to create and manage catalogs of IT services that you have approved for use on AWS, including virtual machine images, servers, software, and databases to complete multi-tier application architectures.

AWS Service Catalog allows you to centrally manage commonly deployed IT services, and helps you achieve consistent governance to meet your compliance requirements, while enabling users to quickly deploy the approved IT services they need.

AMAZON GUARDDUTY   *DOG, threat detection*

Amazon GuardDuty offers threat detection and continuous security monitoring for malicious or unauthorized behavior to help you protect your AWS accounts and workloads.

The service monitors for activity that indicate a possible account compromise, potentially compromised instance, or reconnaissance by attackers or intellectual property, and continuously monitors data access activity for anomalies that might single unauthorized access or inadvertent data leaks.

AWS WAF & AWS SHIELD

AWS WAF

AWS WAF is a web application firewall.

Protects against common exploits that could compromise application availability, compromise security or consume excessive resources.

AWS SHIELD   *- DDoS*   *CloudFront also has DDoS*

AWS Shield is a managed Distributed Denial of Service (DDoS) protection service.

Safeguards web application running on AWS with always-on detection and automatic inline mitigations.

Helps to minimize application downtime and latency.

Two tiers – Standard and Advanced.

AWS KEY MANAGEMENT SERVICE (KMS)   *Key*

AWS Key Management Service gives you centralized control over the encryption keys used to protect your data.

You can create, import, rotate, disable, delete, define usage policies for, and audit the use of encryption keys used to encrypt your data.

AWS Key Management Service is integrated with most other AWS services making it easy to encrypt the data you store in these services with encryption keys you control.

AWS KMS is integrated with AWS CloudTrail which provides you the ability to audit who used which keys, on which resources and when.

AWS KMS enables developers to easily encrypt data, whether through 1-click encryption in the AWS Management Console or using the AWS SDK to easily add encryption in their application code. For more details, visit https://aws.amazon.com/kms/features/

AWS CLOUDHSM   *you manage*

AWS CloudHSM is a cloud-based hardware security module (HSM) that enables you to easily generate and use your own encryption keys on the AWS Cloud.

With CloudHSM, you can manage your own encryption keys using FIPS 140-2 Level 3 validated HSMs.

CloudHSM offers you the flexibility to integrate with your applications using industry-standard APIs, such as PKCS#11, Java Cryptography Extensions (JCE), and Microsoft CryptoNG (CNG) libraries. For more details, visit https://aws.amazon.com/cloudhsm/features/

AWS ARTIFACT   *— compliance certs (SOC, etc.)*

AWS Artifact is your go-to, central resource for compliance-related information that matters to you.

It provides on-demand access to AWS' security and compliance reports and select online agreements.

Reports available in AWS Artifact include the Service Organization Control (SOC) reports, Payment Card Industry (PCI) reports, and certifications from accreditation bodies across geographies and compliance verticals that validate the implementation and operating effectiveness of AWS security controls.

Agreements available in AWS Artifact include the Business Associate Addendum (BAA) and the Nondisclosure Agreement (NDA). For more details, visit:

https://aws.amazon.com/artifact/

AWS INSPECTOR AND AWS TRUSTED ADVISOR

AWS INSPECTOR

- Inspector is an automated security assessment service that helps improve the security and compliance of applications deployed on AWS.
- Inspector automatically assesses applications for vulnerabilities or deviations from best practices.
- Uses an agent installed on EC2 instances.
- Instances must be tagged.

AWS TRUSTED ADVISOR:

- Trusted Advisor is an online resource that helps to reduce cost, increase performance and improve security by optimizing your AWS environment.

- Trusted Advisor provides real time guidance to help you provision your resources following best practices.
- Advisor will advise you on Cost Optimization, Performance, Security, and Fault Tolerance.

Trusted Advisor scans your AWS infrastructure and compares is to AWS best practices in five categories:

- Cost Optimization
- Performance
- Security
- Fault Tolerance
- Service Limits

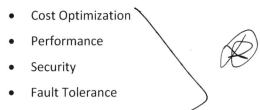

Trusted Advisor comes in two versions: **Core Checks** and **Recommendations** (free).

- Access to the 7 core checks to help increase security and performance.
- Checks include S3 bucket permissions, Security Groups, IAM use, MFA on root account, EBS public snapshots, RDS public snapshots.

Full Trusted Advisor Benefits (business and enterprise support plans):

- Full set of checks to help optimize your entire AWS infrastructure.
- Advises on security, performance, cost, fault tolerance and service limits.
- Additional benefits include weekly update notifications, alerts, automated actions with CloudWatch and programmatic access using the AWS Support API.

AWS PERSONAL HEALTH DASHBOARD   when AWS is having issues

AWS Personal Health Dashboard provides alerts and remediation guidance when AWS is experiencing events that may impact you.

Personal Health Dashboard gives you a personalized view into the performance and availability of the AWS services underlying your AWS resources.

The dashboard displays relevant and timely information to help you manage events in progress.

Also provides proactive notification to help you plan for scheduled activities.

Alerts are triggered by changes in the health of AWS resources, giving you event visibility, and guidance to help quickly diagnose and resolve issues.

You get a personalized view of the status of the AWS services that power your applications, enabling you to quickly see when AWS is experiencing issues that may impact you.

Also provides forward looking notifications, and you can set up alerts across multiple channels, including email and mobile notifications, so you receive timely and relevant information to help plan for scheduled changes that may affect you.

Alerts include remediation details and specific guidance to enable you to take immediate action to address AWS events impacting your resources.

Can integrate with Amazon CloudWatch Events, enabling you to build custom rules and select targets such as AWS Lambda functions to define automated remediation actions.

The AWS Health API allows you to integrate health data and notifications with your existing in-house or third-party IT Management tools.

PENETRATION TESTING

Penetration testing is the practice of testing one's own application's security for vulnerabilities by simulating an attack.

AWS allows penetration testing. There is a limited set of resources on which penetration testing can be performed.

You do not need permission to perform penetration testing against the following services:

- Amazon EC2 instances, NAT Gateways, and Elastic Load Balancers

- Amazon RDS

- Amazon CloudFront

- Amazon Aurora

- Amazon API Gateways

- AWS Lambda and Lambda Edge functions

- Amazon Lightsail resources

- Amazon Elastic Beanstalk environments

You can read the full vulnerability and penetration testing support policy here: https://aws.amazon.com/security/penetration-testing/.

In case an account is or may be compromised, AWS recommend that the following steps are taken:

- Change your AWS root account password.

- Change all IAM user's passwords.

- Delete or rotate all programmatic (API) access keys.

- Delete any resources in your account that you did not create.

- Respond to any notifications you received from AWS through the AWS Support Center and/or contact AWS Support to open a support case.

CLOUD SECURITY QUIZ QUESTIONS

Answers and explanations are provided below after the last question in this section.

Question 1: Which tool can be used to find compliance information that relates to the AWS Cloud platform?

A. Amazon Inspector

B. AWS Trusted Advisor

C. AWS Artifact

D. AWS Personal Health Dashboard

Question 2: What is AWS' policy regarding penetration testing?

A. You can only perform penetration testing with permission from AWS

B. You can perform penetration testing against any service and account

C. You can perform penetration testing against selected services without approval

D. Penetration testing is not allowed under any circumstance

Question 3: Which service can assist with protecting against common web-based exploits?

A. AWS Shield

B. AWS Web Application Firewall (WAF)

C. Amazon Route 53

D. AWS CloudHSM

Question 4: Which service provides guidance for remediation when AWS is experiencing events that may impact you?

A. AWS Trusted Advisor

B. Amazon Inspector

C. AWS Personal Health Dashboard

D. AWS Cloud Compliance

Question 5: Which service is involved with encryption?

A. AWS Key Management Service (KMS)

B. AWS WAF

C. AWS Shield

Question 6: AWS Trusted advisor does NOT provide advice on which of the following?

A. Cost optimization

B. Performance

C. Total Cost of Ownership (TCO)

D. Security

E. Fault Tolerance

Question 7: In case of account compromize, which of actions should you perform?

A. Delete all IAM users

B. Delete all resources in your account

C. Open a support case with AWS

D. Immediately close your account

Question 8: According to the AWS Shared Responsibility model, who is responsible for data center security?

A. AWS

B. The customer

Question 9: Which service uses a hardware security module to protect encryption keys in the cloud?

A. AWS Key Management Service (KMS)

B. AWS CloudHSM

C. AWS Service Catalog

Question 10: Which service can be used to find reports on Payment Card Industry (PCI) compliance of the AWS cloud?

A. AWS Service Catalog

B. Amazon Inspector

C. AWS Artifact

CLOUD SECURITY ANSWERS

Question 1, Answer: C

Explanation:

A is incorrect. Inspector is an automated security assessment service that helps improve the security and compliance of applications deployed on AWS.

B is incorrect. Trusted Advisor is an online resource that helps to reduce cost, increase performance and improve security by optimizing your AWS environment.

C is correct. AWS Artifact is your go-to, central resource for compliance-related information that matters to you. It provides on-demand access to AWS' security and compliance reports and select online agreements.

D is incorrect. AWS Personal Health Dashboard provides alerts and remediation guidance when AWS is experiencing events that may impact you.

Question 2, Answer: C

Explanation:

A is incorrect. This is no longer true, you can now perform penetration testing against selected resources without approval.

B is incorrect. This is not true. You cannot perform penetration testing against all services or against resources in other accounts.

C is correct. This is the new policy. You can now perform penetration testing against several services without approval.

Question 3, Answer: B

Explanation:

A is incorrect. AWS Shield is used for preventing DDoS attacks.

B is correct. AWS WAF is a web application firewall that protects against common exploits that could compromise application availability, compromise security or consume excessive resources.

C is incorrect. Amazon Route 53 performs DNS services, health checking services, and domain registration.

D is incorrect. AWS CloudHSM is a cloud-based hardware security module (HSM) that enables you to easily generate and use your own encryption keys on the AWS Cloud.

Question 4, Answer: C

Explanation:

A is incorrect. Trusted Advisor is an online resource that helps to reduce cost, increase performance and improve security by optimizing your AWS environment. It does not provide remediation guidance when the platform is experiencing technical difficulties.

B is incorrect. Inspector is an automated security assessment service that helps improve the security and compliance of applications deployed on AWS.

C is correct. AWS Personal Health Dashboard provides alerts and remediation guidance when AWS is experiencing events that may impact you. Personal Health Dashboard gives you a personalized view into the performance and availability of the AWS services underlying your AWS resources.

D is incorrect. AWS Cloud Compliance is not a service.

Question 5, Answer: A

Explanation:

A is correct. AWS KMS is used for managing encryption keys.

B is incorrect. AWS Web Application Firewall protects web applications from common exploits.

C is incorrect. AWS Shield helps protect your resources from DDoS attacks.

Question 6, Answer: C

Explanation:

A is incorrect. AWS Trusted advisor does provide advice on cost optimization.

B is incorrect. AWS Trusted advisor does provide advice on performance.

C is correct. AWS Trusted advisor does not provide advice on TCO.

D is incorrect. AWS Trusted advisor does provide advice on security.

E is incorrect. AWS Trusted advisor does provide advice on fault tolerance.

Question 7, Answer: C

Explanation:

A is incorrect. You do not need to delete all IAM users, but you should reset their passwords and delete or rotate API keys.

B is incorrect. You do not need to delete all resources in your account, but you should delete any resources you did not create.

C is correct. You should always respond to any notifications you received from AWS through the AWS Support Center and/or contact AWS Support to open a support case.

D is incorrect. This is unnecessary. You should follow the guidance for how to secure your account.

Question 8, Answer: A

Explanation:

A is correct. AWS is responsible for security "of" the cloud, this includes the facilities in which the services run.

B is incorrect. The customer is not responsible for the data center facilities in which AWS services run.

Question 9, Answer: B

Explanation:

A is incorrect. AWS KMS is a shared service and does not use a hardware security module.

B is correct. AWS CloudHSM is a cloud-based hardware security module (HSM) that enables you to easily generate and use your own encryption keys on the AWS Cloud.

C is incorrect. AWS Service Catalog allows you to centrally manage commonly deployed IT services, and helps you achieve consistent governance to meet your compliance requirements, while enabling users to quickly deploy the approved IT services they need.

D is incorrect.

Question 10, Answer: C

Explanation:

A is incorrect. AWS Service Catalog allows you to centrally manage commonly deployed IT services, and helps you achieve consistent governance to meet your compliance requirements, while enabling users to quickly deploy the approved IT services they need.

B is incorrect. Inspector is an automated security assessment service that helps improve the security and compliance of applications deployed on AWS.

C is correct. AWS Artifact is your go-to, central resource for compliance-related information that matters to you. It provides on-demand access to AWS' security and compliance reports and select online agreements.

SHARED RESPONSIBILITY MODEL

The AWS shared responsibility model defines what you (as an AWS account holder/user) and AWS are responsible for when it comes to security and compliance.

Security and Compliance is a shared responsibility between AWS and the customer. This shared model can help relieve customers' operational burdens as AWS operates, manages and controls the components from the host operating system and virtualization layer down to the physical security of the facilities in which the service operates.

The customer assumes responsibility and management of the guest operating system (including updates and security patches), other associated application software as well as the configuration of the AWS provided security group firewall.

AWS are responsible for "**Security OF the Cloud**".

- AWS is responsible for protecting the infrastructure that runs all of the services offered in the AWS Cloud.

- This infrastructure is composed of the hardware, software, networking, and facilities that run AWS Cloud services.

Customers are responsible for "**Security IN the Cloud**".

- For EC2 this includes network level security (NACLs, security groups), operating system patches and updates, IAM user access management, and client and server-side data encryption.

The following diagram shows the **split of responsibilities between AWS and the customer**:

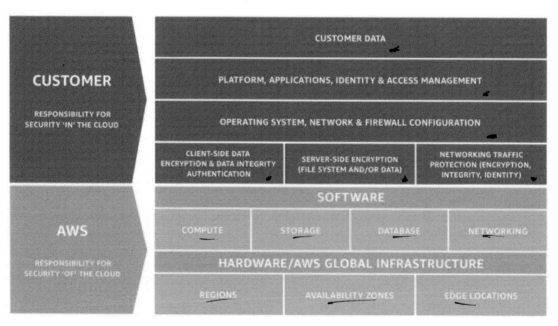

Inherited Controls – Controls which a customer fully inherits from AWS.

- Physical and Environmental controls.

Shared Controls – Controls which apply to both the infrastructure layer and customer layers, but in completely separate contexts or perspectives.

In the AWS shared security model (shared control) AWS provides the requirements for the infrastructure and the customer must provide their own control implementation within their use of AWS services.

Examples of shared controls include:

- **Patch Management** – AWS is responsible for patching and fixing flaws within the infrastructure, but customers are responsible for patching their guest OS and applications.

- **Configuration Management** – AWS maintains the configuration of its infrastructure devices, but a customer is responsible for configuring their own guest operating systems, databases, and applications.

- **Awareness & Training** – AWS trains AWS employees, but a customer must train their own employees.

Customer Specific – Controls which are solely the responsibility of the customer based on the application they are deploying within AWS services.

Examples of customer specific controls include:

- Service and Communications Protection or Zone Security which may require a customer to route or zone data within specific security environments.

SHARED RESPONSIBILITY MODEL QUIZ QUESTIONS

Answers and explanations are provided below after the last question in this section.

Question 1: According to the AWS Shared Responsibility model, who is responsible for operating system patching for Amazon EC2 instances?

A. AWS

B. The Customer

Question 2: According to the AWS Shared Responsibility model, who is responsible for configuring server-side encryption for Amazon S3?

A. AWS

B. The Customer

SHARED RESPONSIBILITY MODEL ANSWERS

Question 1, Answer: B

Explanation:

A is incorrect. AWS is not responsible for operating system patches on EC2 instances.

B is correct. As a customer, you are responsible for installing patches on the operating systems of your EC2 instances.

Question 2, Answer: B

Explanation:

A is incorrect. AWS are not responsible for configuring server-side encryption. It is up to customers to encrypt their data.

B is correct. AWS are not responsible for configuring server-side encryption. It is up to customers to encrypt their data.

ARCHITECTING FOR THE CLOUD

THE CLOUD COMPUTING DIFFERENCE

Architecting for the Cloud is one of the key subjects tested on the Cloud Practitioner exam. The information on this page has been extracted from the **AWS whitepaper "Architecting for The Cloud: Best Practices"** which can be found here:

https://aws.amazon.com/whitepapers/architecting-for-the-aws-cloud-best-practices/

Also, please read the AWS Blog article: **"The 5 Pillars of the AWS Well-Architected Framework"** which can be found here: https://aws.amazon.com/blogs/apn/the-5-pillars-of-the-aws-well-architected-framework/

Cloud computing differs from a traditional environment in the following ways:

IT ASSETS BECOME PROGRAMMABLE RESOURCES

or Provisioned

On AWS, servers, databases, storage and higher-level application components can be instantiated within seconds.

You can treat these as temporary and disposable resources, free from the inflexibility and constraints of a fixed and finite IT infrastructure.

This resets the way you approach change management, testing, reliability and capacity planning.

GLOBAL, AVAILABLE AND UNLIMITED CAPACITY

Using the global infrastructure of AWS, you can deploy your application to the AWS Region that best meets your requirements.

For global applications, you can reduce latency to end users around the world by using the Amazon CloudFront content delivery network.

It is also much easier to operate production applications and databases across multiple data centers to achieve high availability and fault tolerance.

HIGHER LEVEL MANAGED SERVICES

AWS customers also have access to a broad set of compute, storage, database, analytics, application, and deployment services.

These services are instantly available to developers and can reduce dependency on in-house specialized skills and allow organizations to deliver new solutions faster.

These services are managed by AWS, which can lower operational complexity and cost.

SECURITY BUILT-IN

The AWS cloud provides governance capabilities that enable continuous monitoring of configuration changes to your IT resources.

Since AWS assets are programmable resources, your security policy can be formalized and embedded with the design of your infrastructure.

DESIGN PRINCIPLES

SCALABILITY

Systems that are expected to grow over time need to be built on top of a scalable architecture.

Scaling Vertically

Scaling vertically takes place through an increase in the specifications of an individual resource (e.g., upgrading a server with a larger hard drive or a faster CPU).

On Amazon EC2, this can easily be achieved by stopping an instance and resizing it to an instance type that has more RAM, CPU, IO or networking capabilities.

Scaling Horizontally

Scaling horizontally takes place through an increase in the number of resources (e.g., adding more hard drives to a storage array or adding more servers to support an application).

This is a great way to build Internet-scale applications that leverage the elasticity of cloud computing.

The table below provides more information on the **differences between horizontal and vertical scaling**:

Horizontal Scaling	Vertical Scaling
Add more instances as demand increases	Add more CPU and/or RAM to existing instances as demand increases
No downtime required to scale up or down	Requires a restart to scale up or down
Automatic using services such as AWS Auto-Scaling	Would require scripting or automation tools to automate
Unlimited scalability	Scalability limited by maximum instance size

stop, increase, restart

Stateless applications:

- A stateless application is an application that needs no knowledge of previous interactions and stores no session information.

- A stateless application can scale horizontally since any request can be serviced by any of the available compute resources (e.g., EC2 instances, AWS Lambda functions).

Stateless components:

- Most applications need to maintain some kind of state information.

- For example, web applications need to track whether a user is signed in, or else they might present personalized content based on previous actions.

- Web applications can use HTTP cookies to store information about a session at the client's browser (e.g., items in the shopping cart).

- Consider only storing a unique session identifier in a HTTP cookie and storing more detailed user session information server-side.

- DynamoDB is often used for storing session state to maintain a stateless architecture.

- For larger files, a shared storage system can be used such as S3 or EFS.

- SWF can be used for a multi-step workflow.

Stateful components:

- Databases are stateful.

- Many legacy applications are stateful.

- Load balancing with session affinity can be used for horizontal scaling of stateful components.

- Session affinity is however not guaranteed and existing sessions do not benefit from newly launched nodes.

Distributed processing:

- Use cases that involve processing of very large amounts of data (e.g., anything that can't be handled by a single compute resource in a timely manner) require a distributed processing approach.

- By dividing a task and its data into many small fragments of work, you can execute each of them in any of a larger set of available compute resources.

2) DISPOSABLE RESOURCES INSTEAD OF FIXED SERVERS

Think of servers and other components as temporary resources.

Launch as many as you need and use them only for as long as you need them.

An issue with fixed, long-running servers is that of configuration drift (where change and software patches are applied over time).

This problem can be solved with the "immutable infrastructure" pattern where a server is never updated but instead is replaced with a new one as required.

Instantiating compute resources

You don't want to manually set up new resources with their configuration and code.

Use automated, repeatable processes that avoid long lead times and are not prone to human error.

Bootstrapping:

- Execute automated bootstrapping actions to modify default configurations.

- This includes scripts that install software or copy data to bring that resource to a particular state.

- You can parameterize configuration details that vary between different environments.

Golden Images:

- Some resource types can be launched from a golden image. $\searrow$
- Examples are EC2 instances, RDS instances and EBS volumes.
- A golden image is a snapshot of a particular state for that resource.
- Compared to bootstrapping, golden images provide faster start times and remove dependencies to configuration services or third-party repositories.

Infrastructure are Code:

- AWS assets are programmable, so you can apply techniques, practices and tools from software development to make your whole infrastructure reusable, maintainable, extensible and testable.

AUTOMATION → Serverless

In a traditional IT infrastructure, you often have to manually react to a variety of events.

When deploying on AWS, there is a lot of opportunity for automation.

This improves both your system's stability and the efficiency of your organization.

Examples of **automations using AWS services** include:

- **AWS Elastic Beanstalk** – the fastest and simplest way to get an application up and running on AWS.
- **Amazon EC2 Auto Recovery** – You can create an Amazon CloudWatch alarm that monitors an Amazon EC2 instance and automatically recovers it if it becomes impaired.
- **Auto Scaling** – With Auto Scaling, you can maintain application availability and scale your Amazon EC2 capacity up or down automatically according to conditions you define.
- **Amazon CloudWatch Alarms** – You can create a CloudWatch alarm that sends an Amazon Simple Notification Service (Amazon SNS) message when a particular metric goes beyond a specified threshold for a specified number of periods.
- **Amazon CloudWatch Events** – The CloudWatch service delivers a near real-time stream of system events that describe changes in AWS resources.
- **AWS OpsWorks Lifecycle Events** – AWS OpsWorks supports continuous configuration through lifecycle events that automatically update your instances' configuration to adapt to environment changes.
- **AWS Lambda Scheduled Events** – These events allow you to create a Lambda function and direct AWS Lambda to execute it on a regular schedule.

LOOSE COUPLING

As application complexity increases, a desirable attribute of an IT system is that it can be broken into smaller, loosely coupled components.

This means that IT systems should be designed in a way that reduces interdependencies – a change or a failure in one component should <u>not</u> cascade to other components.

Design principles include:

- **Well-defined interfaces** – reduce interdependencies in a system by enabling interaction only through specific, technology-agnostic interfaces (e.g., RESTful APIs).

- **Service discovery** – disparate resources must have a way of discovering each other without prior knowledge of the network topology.

- **Asynchronous integration** – this is another form of loose coupling where an interaction does not need an immediate response (think SQS queue or Kinesis).

- **Graceful failure** – build applications such that they handle failure in a graceful manner (reduce the impact of failure and implement retries).

5 SERVICES, NOT SERVERS

With traditional IT infrastructure, organizations have to build and operate a wide variety of technology components.

AWS offers a broad set of compute, storage, database, analytics, application, and deployment services that help organizations move faster and lower IT costs.

Managed services:

- On AWS, there is a set of services that provide building blocks that developers can consume to power their applications.

- These managed services include databases, machine learning, analytics, queuing, search, email, notifications and more.

Serverless architectures:

- Another approach that can reduce the operational complexity of running applications is that of the serverless architectures.

- It is possible to build both event-driven and synchronous services for mobile, web, analytics and the Internet of Things (IoT) without managing any server infrastructure.

6 DATABASES

With traditional IT infrastructure, organizations were often limited to the database and storage technologies they could use.

With AWS, these constraints are removed by managed database services that offer enterprise performance at open source cost.

Relational Databases   vertical scaling

Relational databases (often called RDBS or SQL databases) normalize data into well-defined tabular structures known as tables, which consist of rows and columns.

They provide a powerful query language, flexible indexing capabilities, strong integrity controls and the ability to combine data from multiple tables in a fast and efficient manner.

Amazon RDS is a relational database service.

Scalability:

- Relational databases can scale vertically (e.g., upgrading to a larger RDS DB instance).

- For read-heavy use cases, you can scale horizontally using read replicas.

- For scaling write capacity beyond a single instance data partitioning or sharding is required.

High Availability:

- For production DBs, Amazon recommend the use of RDS Multi-AZ which creates a synchronously replicated standby in another AZ.

- With Multi-AZ RDS can failover to the standby node without administrative intervention.

Anti-Patterns:

- If your application primarily indexes and queries data with no need for joins or complex transactions, consider a NoSQL database instead.

- If you have large binary files (audio, video and image), it will be more efficient to store the actual files in S3 and only hold the metadata for the files in your database.

NoSQL Databases   *horizontal scaling*

NoSQL is a term used to describe databases that trade some of the query and transaction capabilities of relational databases for a more flexible data model that seamlessly scales horizontally.

NoSQL databases utilize a variety of data models, including graphs, key-value pairs, and JSON documents.

DynamoDB is Amazon's NoSQL database service.

Scalability:

- NoSQL database engines will typically perform data partitioning and replication to scale both the reads and the writes in a horizontal fashion.

High Availability:

- DynamoDB synchronously replicates data across three facilities in an AWS region for fault tolerance.

Anti-Patterns:

- If your schema cannot be denormalized and your application requires joins or complex transactions, consider a relational database instead.

- If you have large binary files (audio, video, and image), consider storing the files in Amazon S3 and storing the metadata for the files in your database.

Data Warehouse   *Redshift*

A data warehouse is a specialized type of relational database, optimized for analysis and reporting of large amounts of data.

It can be used to combine transactional data from disparate sources making them available for analysis and decision-making.

Amazon Redshift is a managed data warehouse service that is designed to operate at less than a tenth the cost of traditional solutions.

Scalability:

Graph Database = Neptune

- Amazon Redshift achieves efficient storage and optimum query performance through a combination of massively parallel processing (MPP), columnar data storage, and targeted data compression encoding schemes.

- RedShift is particularly suited to analytic and reporting workloads against very large data sets.

High Availability:

- Redshift has multiple features that enhance the reliability of your data warehouse cluster.

- Multi-node clusters replicate data to other nodes within the cluster.

- Data is continuously backed up to S3.

- RedShift continuously monitors the health of the cluster and re-replicates data from failed drives and replaces nodes as necessary.

Anti-Patterns:

- Because Amazon Redshift is a SQL-based relational database management system (RDBMS), it is compatible with other RDBMS applications and business intelligence tools.

- Although Amazon Redshift provides the functionality of a typical RDBMS, including online transaction processing (OLTP) functions, it is not designed for these workloads.

Search

Applications that require sophisticated search functionality will typically outgrow the capabilities of relational or NoSQL databases.

A search service can be used to index and search both structured and free text format and can support functionality that is not available in other databases, such as customizable result ranking, faceting for filtering, synonyms, stemming, etc.

Scalability:

- Both Amazon CloudSearch and Amazon ES use data partitioning and replication to scale horizontally.

High Availability:

- Both services provide features that store data redundantly across Availability Zones.

REMOVING SINGLE POINTS OF FAILURE

A system is highly available when it can withstand the failure of an individual or multiple components.

Automate recovery and reduce disruption at every layer of your architecture.

Introducing Redundancy

Single points of failure can be removed by introducing redundancy.

In standby redundancy, when a resource fails, functionality is recovered on a secondary resource using a process called failover, which typically take some time to complete.

In active redundancy, requests are distributed to multiple redundant compute resources, and when one of them fails, the rest can simply absorb a larger share of the workload.

Detect Failure

Build as much automation as possible in both detecting and reacting to failure.

Services like ELB and Route53 mask failure by routing traffic to a healthy endpoint.

Auto Scaling can be configured to automatically replace unhealthy nodes.

You can also replace unhealthy nodes using the EC2 auto- recovery, OpsWorks and Elastic Beanstalk.

Durable Data Storage

Design your architecture to protect both data availability and integrity.

Data replication is the technique that introduces redundant copies of data.

It can help horizontally scale read capacity, but can also increase data durability and availability.

Replication can take place in a few different modes:

- **Synchronous replication** – transactions are acknowledged only after data has been durably stored in both the primary and replica instance. Can be used to protect data integrity (low RPO) and scaling read capacity (with strong consistency).

- **Asynchronous replication** – changes on the primary node are not immediately reflected on its replicas. Can be used to horizontally scale the system's read capacity (with replication lag) and data durability (with some data loss).

- Quorum-based replication – combines synchronous and asynchronous replication and is good for large-scale distributed database systems.

Automated Multi-Data Center Resilience

With traditional infrastructure, failing over between data centers is performed using a disaster recovery plan.

Long distances between data centers mean that latency makes synchronous replication impractical.

Failovers often lead to data loss and costly data recovery processes.

On AWS it is possible to adopt a simpler, more efficient protection from this type of failure.

Each AWS region contains multiple distinct locations called Availability Zones (AZs).

Each AZ is engineered to be isolated from failures in other AZs.

An AZ is a data center and, in some cases, an AZ consists of multiple data centers.

AZs within a region provide inexpensive, low-latency network connectivity to other zones in the same region.

This allows you to replicate your data across data centers in a synchronous manner so that failover can be automated and be transparent for your users.

Fault Isolation and Traditional Horizontal Scaling

Though the active redundancy pattern is great for balancing traffic and handling instance or Availability Zone disruptions, it is not sufficient if there is something harmful about the requests themselves.

If a particular request happens to trigger a bug that causes the system to fail over, then the caller may trigger a cascading failure by repeatedly trying the same request against all instances.

One fault-isolating improvement you can make to traditional horizontal scaling is called sharding.

Similar to the technique traditionally used with data storage systems, instead of spreading traffic from all customers across every node, you can group the instances into shards.

In this way, you are able to reduce the impact on customers in direct proportion to the number of shards you have.

Optimize for Cost

Just by moving existing architectures into the cloud, organizations can reduce capital expenses and drive savings as a result of the AWS economies of scale.

By iterating and making use of more AWS capabilities there is further opportunity to create cost-optimized cloud architectures.

Right Sizing:

- In some cases, you should select the cheapest type that suits your workload's requirements.
- In other cases, using fewer instances of a larger instance type might result in lower total cost or better performance.
- Benchmark and select the right instance type depending on how your workload utilizes CPU, RAM, network, storage size and I/O.
- Reduce cost by selecting the right storage solution for your needs.
- E.g., S3 offers a variety of storage classes, including Standard, Reduced Redundancy, and Standard-Infrequent Access.
- EC2, RDS and ES support different EBS volume types (magnetic, general purpose SSD, provisioned IOPS SSD) that you should evaluate.

Elasticity:

- Plan to implement Auto Scaling for as many EC2 workloads as possible, so that you horizontally scale up when needed and scale down automatically to reduce cost.
- Automate turning off non-production workloads when not in use.
- Where possible, replace EC2 workloads with AWS managed services that don't require you to take any capacity decisions. For example:
    - ELB
    - CloudFront
    - SQS
    - Kinesis Firehose
    - Lambda
    - SES
    - CloudSearch
- Or use services for which you can modify capacity as required. For example:

- DynamoDB
- RDS
- Elasticsearch Service

Take Advantage of the variety of Purchasing Options:

- EC2 On-Demand instance pricing gives you maximum flexibility with no long-term commitments.

- There are two more ways to pay for Amazon EC2 instances that can help you reduce spend: Reserved Instances and Spot Instances.

Reserved Capacity

EC2 Reserved Instances allow you to reserve Amazon EC2 computing capacity in exchange for a significantly discounted hourly rate compared to On-Demand instance pricing.

This is ideal for applications with predictable minimum capacity requirements.

Spot Instances

For less steady workloads, you can consider the use of Spot Instances.

EC2 Spot Instances allow you to bid on spareEC2 computing capacity.

Since Spot Instances are often available at a discount compared to On-Demand pricing, you can significantly reduce the cost of running your applications.

Spot Instances are ideal for workloads that have flexible start and end times.

If the Spot market price increases above your bid price, your instance will be terminated automatically, and you will not be charged for the partial hour that your instance has run.

As a result, Spot Instances are great for workloads that have tolerance to interruption.

CACHING

Caching is a technique that stores previously calculated data for future use.

This technique is used to improve application performance and increase the cost efficiency of an implementation.

It can be applied at multiple layers of an IT architecture.

Application Data Caching   *Elasticache*

Applications can be designed so that they store and retrieve information from fast, managed, in-memory caches.

Cached information may include the results of I/O-intensive database queries or the outcome of computationally intensive processing.

Edge Caching   *CDN*

Copies of static content and dynamic content can be cached at Amazon CloudFront, which is a content delivery network (CDN) consisting of multiple edge locations around the world.

Edge caching allows content to be served by infrastructure that is closer to viewers, lowering latency and giving you the high, sustained data transfer rates needed to deliver large popular objects to end users at scale.

9) SECURITY

Most of the security tools and techniques that you might already be familiar with in a traditional IT infrastructure can be used in the cloud.

At the same time, AWS allows you to improve your security in a variety of ways.

AWS is a platform that allows you to formalize the design of security controls in the platform itself.

Utilize AWS Features for Defense in Depth

Network level security includes building a VPC topology that isolates parts of the infrastructure through the use of subnets, security groups, and routing controls.

Services like AWS WAF, a web application firewall, can help protect web applications from SQL injection and other vulnerabilities in application code.

For access control, you can use IAM to define a granular set of policies and assign them to users, groups and AWS resources.

Finally, the AWS platform offers a breadth of options for protecting data, whether it is in transit or at rest with encryption.

Offload Security Responsibility to AWS

AWS operates under a shared security responsibility model, where AWS is responsible for the security of the underlying cloud infrastructure and you are responsible for securing the workloads you deploy in AWS.

Reduce Privileged Access   = Least Priv Acces

When you treat servers as programmable resources, you can capitalize on that for benefits in the security space as well.

Eliminate the need for guest operating system access to production environments.

If an instance experiences an issue you can automatically or manually terminate and replace it.

In a traditional environment, service accounts would often be assigned long-term credentials stored in a configuration file.

On AWS, you can instead use IAM roles to grant permissions to applications running on Amazon EC2 instances through the use of short-term credentials.

Security as Code

Traditional security frameworks, regulations and organizational policies define security requirements related to things such as firewall rules, network access controls, internal/external subnets and operating system hardening.

You can implement these in an AWS environment as well, but you now have the opportunity to capture them all in a script that defines a "Golden Environment."

This means you can create an AWS CloudFormation script that captures your security policy and reliably deploys it.

Security best practices can now be reused among multiple projects and become part of your continuous integration pipeline.

You can perform security testing as part of your release cycle and automatically discover application gaps and drift from your security policy.

Real-Time Auditing

Testing and auditing your environment are key to moving fast while staying safe.

Traditional approaches that involve periodic checks are not sufficient, especially in agile environments where change is constant.

On AWS, it is possible to implement continuous monitoring and automation of controls to minimize exposure to security risks.

Services like AWS Config, Amazon Inspector and AWS Trusted Advisor continually monitor for compliance or vulnerabilities.

With AWS Config rules, you will also know if some component was out of compliance even for a brief period of time.

You can implement extensive logging for your applications (using Amazon CloudWatch Logs) and for the actual AWS API calls by enabling AWS CloudTrail.

Logs can then be stored in an immutable manner and automatically processed to either notify or even take action on your behalf, protecting your organization from non-compliance.   53

You can use AWS Lambda, Amazon EMR, the Amazon Elasticsearch Service, or third- party tools from the AWS Marketplace to scan logs to detect things like unused permissions, overuse of privileged accounts, usage of keys, anomalous logins, policy violations and system abuse.

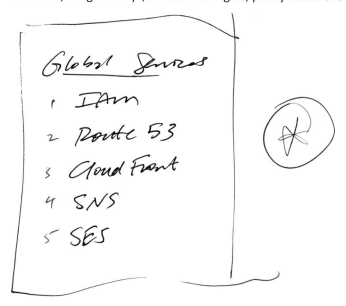

ARCHITECTING FOR THE CLOUD QUIZ QUESTIONS

Answers and explanations are provided below after the last question in this section.

Question 1: Which architectural benefit of the AWS Cloud assists with lowering operational cost?

A. Higher-level managed services   *less employee experience req'd*

B. Horizontal scaling

C. Loose coupling

D. Design for failure

Question 2: AWS EC2 Auto Scaling provides which type of scaling?

A. Horizontal

B. Vertical

Question 3: Which type of scaling does an Amazon Read Replica provide?

A. Horizontal

B. Vertical

Question 4: Which of the following is a benefit of API-driven services?

A. You can programmatically and dynamically launch resources

B. You can define services through the AWS management console

C. You get greater fault tolerance

D. Increased reliability

Question 5: Which of the following is an architectural best practice?

A. Design for the future

B. Design monolithic applications

C. Design for failure

D. Use close coupling

Question 6: The best practice "services, not servers" means what?

A. You should try to use more services such as managed services and serverless services

B. You should not use servers such as Amazon EC2

C. Try to only use serverless services

Question 7: How does DynamoDB scale?   *nosqu*

A. Vertically

(B) Horizontally

C. Both vertically and horizontally

Question 8: Which architectural best practice aims to reduce interdependencies between application components?

A. Automation

B. Services, Not Servers

C. Removing Single Points of Failure

(D) Loose Coupling

Question 9: Which of the following is NOT a limitation of scaling vertically?

A. Can reach a limit of maximum instance size

B. Often requires manual intervention

C. Requires a load balancer for distributing load

D. Typically requires downtime

Question 10: Which services can scale horizontally?

A. Amazon DynamoDB, Amazon EC2 Auto Scaling, Amazon S3

B. Amazon DynamoDB, Amazon EFS, Amazon EC2

C. Amazon EC2 Auto Scaling, Amazon S3, NAT Instance

Question 11: If using a well written template, how can Amazon CloudFront assist with building secure environments?

A. It does not require privileged access

(B) It ensures consistent builds when building repeatably

C. The responsibility is shared with AWS

Question 12: Who is responsible for patching networking equipment in AWS?

(A) AWS

B. The Customer

ARCHITECTING FOR THE CLOUD ANSWERS

Question 1, Answer: A

Explanation:

A is correct. You can lower operational cost by leveraging managed storage, database, analytics, application and deployment services.

B is incorrect. This does not reduce operational cost, it makes scaling more seamless and typically allows you to scale with less restriction.

C is incorrect. Loose coupling is a best practice for architectures to reduce interdependencies between systems. This does not necessarily lower operational cost, it's more about creating stable applications that have fault tolerance.

D is incorrect. This is a design best practice that asks architects to consider how applications might fail and include mitigations in their design.

Question 2, Answer: A

Explanation:

A is correct. EC2 Auto Scaling provide horizontal scaling by launching and terminating additional EC2 instances.

B is incorrect. EC2 Auto Scaling does not provide vertical scaling. An example of vertical scaling is changing to a larger instance type.

Question 3, Answer: A

Explanation:

A is incorrect. By offloading reads to another RDS instance you are using horizontal scaling.

B is correct. This is not an example of vertical scaling. With vertical scaling you would be changing the RDS instance type.

Question 4, Answer: A

Explanation:

A is correct. With API driven cloud services you can programmatically and dynamically launch resources.

B is incorrect. Using the AWS management console is not an example of using the API (though of course it does drive AWS through the API).

C is incorrect. This is not the case, you don't need API-driven services for fault tolerance.

D is incorrect. This is not the case, API-driven services don't necessarily increase reliability.

Question 5, Answer: C

Explanation:

A is incorrect. This is not a best practice that AWS discuss, though of course you should plan for growth.

B is incorrect. This is not a best practice. With cloud applications, architects typically prefer microservice architectures without monolithic stacks.

C is correct. This is an architectural best practice. You should always consider what might fail and ensure the application architecture can mitigate the impact of any failure.

D is incorrect. Close coupling is not an architectural best practice. Loose coupling is a best practice that aims to reduce interdependencies between application components.

Question 6, Answer: A

Explanation:

A is correct. This best practices advises customers to leverage more than just Amazon EC2. Try to use the breadth of services available on AWS.

B is incorrect. This is not the message. However, you should try to use the breadth of services available on AWS.

C is incorrect. This would be hard to achieve and is not the advice here. However, you should try to use the breadth of services available on AWS.

Question 7, Answer: B

Explanation:

A is incorrect. DynamoDB only scales horizontally.

B is correct. DynamoDB does scale horizontally.

C is incorrect. DynamoDB only scales horizontally.

Question 8, Answer: D

Explanation:

A is incorrect. Automation is not about reducing interdependencies between application components.

B is incorrect. Automation is not about reducing interdependencies between application components.

C is incorrect. Automation is not about reducing interdependencies between application components.

D is correct. Design IT systems to reduce interdependencies. A change or a failure in one component should not cascade to other components.

Question 9, Answer: C

Explanation:

A is incorrect. This is a valid limitation of scaling vertically.

B is incorrect. This is a valid limitation of scaling vertically.

C is correct. This is not the case. When scaling EC2 instances horizontally you need a load balancer.

Question 10, Answer: A

Explanation:

A is correct. All of these services scale horizontally.

B is incorrect. Amazon EC2 scales vertically (unless using Auto Scaling).

C is incorrect. A NAT instance runs on Amazon EC2 and you must scale it vertically.

Question 11, Answer: B

Explanation:

A is incorrect. This is not true, you need to have the required privileges to launch each resource.

B is correct. It ensures consistent builds when building repeatably.

C is incorrect. This is not true, you are responsible for resources you launch on AWS.

Question 12, Answer: A

Explanation:

A is correct. AWS are responsible for patching and securing the networking, compute, and storage hardware.

B is incorrect. The customer is not responsible for patching hardware.

ADDITIONAL TOOLS AND SERVICES

There are Additional AWS Services & Tools that may feature on the exam. Often you do not need to know these at a deep level but do need to understand what they are and what they are used for.

What follows are some high-level details and links for more information for some of these services and tools.

Exam tip: Before sitting the exam, it would be wise to go through the AWS console and pick out any services you're not familiar with and do a bit of reading up on them using the AWS documentation.

COMPUTE

Amazon Elastic Container Service for Kubernetes (EKS):   K = Kubernetes

- Amazon Elastic Container Service for Kubernetes (EKS) is a managed Kubernetes service that makes it easy for you to run Kubernetes on AWS without needing to install, operate and maintain your own Kubernetes control plane.

- EKS is certified Kubernetes conformant, so existing applications running on upstream Kubernetes are compatible with Amazon EKS.

- EKS automatically manages the availability and scalability of the Kubernetes control plane nodes that are responsible for starting and stopping containers, scheduling containers on virtual machines, storing cluster data and other tasks.

- EKS automatically detects and replaces unhealthy control plane nodes for each cluster.

- Generally available but only in limited regions currently.

- https://aws.amazon.com/eks/features/

AWS Batch:

- With AWS Batch, you simply package the code for your batch jobs, specify their dependencies and submit your batch job using the AWS Management Console, CLIs, or SDKs.

- AWS Batch allows you to specify execution parameters and job dependencies and facilitates integration with a broad range of popular batch computing workflow engines and languages (e.g., Pegasus WMS, Luigi and AWS Step Functions).

- AWS Batch efficiently and dynamically provisions and scales Amazon EC2 and Spot Instances based on the requirements of your jobs. AWS Batch provides default job queues and compute environment definitions that enable you to get started quickly.

- https://aws.amazon.com/batch/features/

AWS Elastic Beanstalk:

- AWS Elastic Beanstalk is the fastest and simplest way to get web applications up and running on AWS.

- Developers simply upload their application code and the service automatically handles all the details such as resource provisioning, load balancing, auto-scaling and monitoring.

- Elastic Beanstalk is ideal if you have a PHP, Java, Python, Ruby, Node.js, .NET, Go or Docker web application.

- Elastic Beanstalk uses core AWS services such as Amazon EC2, Amazon Elastic Container Service (Amazon ECS), Auto Scaling and Elastic Load Balancing to easily support applications that need to scale to serve millions of users.
- https://aws.amazon.com/elasticbeanstalk/details/

STORAGE

Gateway = on prem

AWS Storage Gateway:

- AWS Storage Gateway is a hybrid cloud storage service that connects your existing on-premises environments with the AWS Cloud.
- Its features make it easy for you to run hybrid cloud workloads at any stage of your cloud adoption, whether it's getting started with cloud backups, running cloud processing workflows for data generated by on-premises machines, or performing a one-time migration of block volume data or databases.
- Storage Gateway seamlessly connects to your local production or backup applications with NFS, SMB, iSCS or iSCSI-VTL, so you can adopt AWS Cloud storage without needing to modify your applications.
- Its protocol conversion and device emulation enables you to access block data on volumes managed by Storage Gateway on top of Amazon S3, store files as native Amazon S3 objects and keep virtual tape backups online in a Virtual Tape Library backed by S3 or move the backups to a tape archive tier on Amazon Glacier.
- https://digitalcloud.training/certification-training/aws-solutions-architect-associate/storage/aws-storage-gateway/
- https://aws.amazon.com/storagegateway/features/

DATABASE

Amazon Elasticache:

- Amazon ElastiCache offers fully managed Redis and Memcached.
- Seamlessly deploy, run and scale popular open source compatible in-memory data stores.
- Amazon ElastiCache can be used to significantly improve latency and throughput for many read-heavy application workloads (such as social networking, gaming, media sharing and Q&A portals) or compute-intensive workloads (such as a recommendation engine) by allowing you to store the objects that are often read in cache.
- Amazon ElastiCache simplifies and offloads the management, monitoring and operation of in-memory cache environments, enabling you to focus on the differentiating parts of your applications.
- Pay only for the resources you consume based on node hours used.
- https://aws.amazon.com/elasticache/features/

Amazon Neptune:

- Amazon Neptune is a fast, reliable, fully-managed graph database service that makes it easy to build and run applications that work with highly connected datasets.

- With Amazon Neptune, you can create sophisticated, interactive graph applications that can query billions of relationships in milliseconds.

- SQL queries for highly connected data are complex and hard to tune for performance. Instead, Amazon Neptune allows you to use the popular graph query languages Apache TinkerPop Gremlin and W3C's SPARQL to execute powerful queries that are easy to write and perform well on connected data.

- https://aws.amazon.com/neptune/features/

MIGRATION

AWS Migration Hub:

- AWS Migration Hub provides a single location to track the progress of application migrations across multiple AWS and partner solutions.

- Using Migration Hub allows you to choose the AWS and partner migration tools that best fit your needs, while providing visibility into the status of migrations across your portfolio of applications.

- For example, you might use AWS Database Migration Service, AWS Server Migration Service, and partner migration tools such as ATADATA ATAmotion, CloudEndure Live Migration or RiverMeadow Server Migration SaaS to migrate an application comprised of a database, virtualized web servers and a bare metal server.

- Using Migration Hub, you can view the migration progress of all the resources in the application.

- https://aws.amazon.com/migration-hub/features/

AWS Database Migration Service:

- AWS Database Migration Service helps you migrate databases to AWS quickly and securely.

- The source database remains fully operational during the migration, minimizing downtime to applications that rely on the database.

- The AWS Database Migration Service can migrate your data to and from most widely used commercial and open-source databases.

- AWS Database Migration Service supports homogenous migrations such as Oracle to Oracle, as well as heterogeneous migrations between different database platforms, such as Oracle or Microsoft SQL Server to Amazon Aurora.

- With AWS Database Migration Service, you can continuously replicate your data with high availability and consolidate databases into a petabyte-scale data warehouse by streaming data to Amazon Redshift and Amazon S3.

- https://aws.amazon.com/dms/

AWS Server Migration Service:

- AWS Server Migration Service (SMS) is an agentless service which makes it easier and faster for you to migrate thousands of on-premises workloads to AWS.

- AWS SMS allows you to automate, schedule, and track incremental replications of live server volumes, making it easier for you to coordinate large-scale server migrations.

- https://aws.amazon.com/server-migration-service/

NETWORKING & CONTENT DELIVERY

Amazon API Gateway:

- Amazon API Gateway is a fully managed service that makes it easy for developers to create, publish, maintain, monitor and secure APIs at any scale.

- With a few clicks in the AWS Management Console, you can create an API that acts as a "front door" for applications to access data, business logic or functionality from your back-end services.

- Back-end services may include Amazon Elastic Compute Cloud (Amazon EC2), code running on AWS Lambda, or any web application.

- https://aws.amazon.com/api-gateway/features/

AWS Direct Connect:

- AWS Direct Connect is a cloud service solution that makes it easy to establish a dedicated network connection from your premises to AWS.

- Using AWS Direct Connect, you can establish private connectivity between AWS and your datacenter, office or colocation environment, which in many cases can reduce your network costs, increase bandwidth throughput and provide a more consistent network experience than Internet-based connections.

- AWS Direct Connect lets you establish a dedicated network connection between your network and one of the AWS Direct Connect locations.

- Using industry standard 802.1q VLANs, this dedicated connection can be partitioned into multiple virtual interfaces.

- This allows you to use the same connection to access public resources such as objects stored in Amazon S3 using public IP address space and private resources such as Amazon EC2 instances running within an Amazon Virtual Private Cloud (VPC) using private IP space, while maintaining network separation between the public and private environments.

- https://aws.amazon.com/directconnect/features/

DEVELOPER TOOLS

AWS CodeStar: _Continuous Delivery_

- AWS CodeStar enables you to quickly develop, build and deploy applications on AWS. AWS CodeStar provides a unified user interface, enabling you to easily manage your software development activities in one place.

- With AWS CodeStar, you can set up your entire continuous delivery toolchain in minutes, allowing you to start releasing code faster. AWS CodeStar makes it easy for your whole team to work together securely, allowing you to easily manage access and add owners, contributors and viewers to your projects.

- With AWS CodeStar, you can use a variety of project templates to start developing applications on Amazon EC2, AWS Lambda and AWS Elastic Beanstalk.

- AWS CodeStar projects support many popular programming languages including Java, JavaScript, PHP, Ruby and Python.

- https://aws.amazon.com/codestar/features/

AWS CodeCommit: *Similar to Git hub*

- AWS CodeCommit is a fully-managed source control service that hosts secure Git-based repositories.

- It makes it easy for teams to collaborate on code in a secure and highly scalable ecosystem.

- CodeCommit eliminates the need to operate your own source control system or worry about scaling its infrastructure.

- You can use CodeCommit to securely store anything from source code to binaries, and it works seamlessly with your existing Git tools.

- https://aws.amazon.com/codecommit/features/

AWS CodeBuild:

- AWS CodeBuild is a fully managed continuous integration service that compiles source code, runs tests and produces software packages that are ready to deploy.

- With CodeBuild, you don't need to provision, manage and scale your own build servers. CodeBuild scales continuously and processes multiple builds concurrently, so your builds are not left waiting in a queue.

- You can get started quickly by using prepackaged build environments, or you can create custom build environments that use your own build tools.

- With CodeBuild, you are charged by the minute for the compute resources you use.

- https://aws.amazon.com/codebuild/features/

AWS CodeDeploy:

- AWS CodeDeploy is a fully managed deployment service that automates software deployments to a variety of compute services such as Amazon EC2, AWS Lambda and your on-premises servers.

- AWS CodeDeploy makes it easier for you to rapidly release new features, helps you avoid downtime during application deployment and handles the complexity of updating your applications.

- You can use AWS CodeDeploy to automate software deployments, eliminating the need for error-prone manual operations. The service scales to match your deployment needs, from a single Lambda function to thousands of EC2 instances.

- https://aws.amazon.com/codedeploy/features/

AWS CodePipeline:

- AWS CodePipeline is a fully managed continuous delivery service that helps you automate your release pipelines for fast and reliable application and infrastructure updates.

- CodePipeline automates the build, test and deploy phases of your release process every time there is a code change, based on the release model you define.

- This enables you to rapidly and reliably deliver features and updates.

- You can easily integrate AWS CodePipeline with third-party services such as GitHub or with your own custom plugin.

- https://aws.amazon.com/codepipeline/features/

AWS X-Ray:

- AWS X-Ray helps developers analyze and debug production, distributed applications, such as those built using a microservices architecture.

- With X-Ray, you can understand how your application and its underlying services are performing to identify and troubleshoot the root cause of performance issues and errors.

- X-Ray provides an end-to-end view of requests as they travel through your application and shows a map of your application's underlying components.

- You can use X-Ray to analyze both applications in development and in production, from simple three-tier applications to complex microservices applications consisting of thousands of services.

- https://aws.amazon.com/xray/features/

MANAGEMENT TOOLS

AWS CloudFormation:

- AWS CloudFormation provides a common language for you to describe and provision all the infrastructure resources in your cloud environment.

- CloudFormation allows you to use a simple text file to model and provision, in an automated and secure manner - all the resources needed for your applications across all regions and accounts.

- This file serves as the single source of truth for your cloud environment.

- You can use JSON or YAML to describe what AWS resources you want to create and configure.

- https://aws.amazon.com/cloudformation/features/

- https://digitalcloud.training/certification-training/aws-solutions-architect-associate/management-tools/aws-cloudformation/

AWS Config:

- AWS Config is a service that enables you to assess, audit and evaluate the configurations of your AWS resources.

- Config continuously monitors and records your AWS resource configurations and allows you to automate the evaluation of recorded configurations against desired configurations.

- With Config, you can review changes in configurations and relationships between AWS resources, dive into detailed resource configuration histories and determine your overall compliance against the configurations specified in your internal guidelines.

- This enables you to simplify compliance auditing, security analysis, change management and operational troubleshooting.

- https://aws.amazon.com/config/features/

AWS OpsWorks:

- AWS OpsWorks is a configuration management service that provides managed instances of Chef and Puppet.

- Chef and Puppet are automation platforms that allow you to use code to automate the configurations of your servers.

- OpsWorks lets you use Chef and Puppet to automate how servers are configured, deployed and managed across your Amazon EC2 instances or on-premises compute environments.

- OpsWorks has three offerings, AWS Opsworks for Chef Automate, AWS OpsWorks for Puppet Enterprise and AWS OpsWorks Stacks

AWS Service Catalog: *Approved for in-house use*

- AWS Service Catalog allows organizations to create and manage catalogs of IT services that are approved for use on AWS.

- These IT services can include everything from virtual machine images, servers, software, and databases to complete multi-tier application architectures.

- AWS Service Catalog allows you to centrally manage commonly deployed IT services, and helps you achieve consistent governance and meet your compliance requirements, while enabling users to quickly deploy only the approved IT services they need.

- Uses CloudFormation templates.

- https://aws.amazon.com/servicecatalog/features/

AWS Systems Manager:

- AWS Systems Manager gives you visibility and control of your infrastructure on AWS.

- Systems Manager provides a unified user interface so you can view operational data from multiple AWS services and allows you to automate operational tasks across your AWS resources.

- With Systems Manager, you can group resources, like Amazon EC2 instances, Amazon S3 buckets, or Amazon RDS instances, by application, view operational data for monitoring and troubleshooting and take action on your groups of resources.

- Systems Manager simplifies resource and application management, shortens the time to detect and resolve operational problems and makes it easy to operate and manage your infrastructure securely at scale.

- https://aws.amazon.com/systems-manager/features/

AWS Managed Services:

- AWS Managed Services provides ongoing management of your AWS infrastructure so you can focus on your applications.

- By implementing best practices to maintain your infrastructure, AWS Managed Services helps to reduce your operational overhead and risk.

- AWS Managed Services automates common activities such as change requests, monitoring, patch management, security and backup services, and provides full-lifecycle services to provision, run and support your infrastructure.
- AWS Managed Services delivers consistent operations management and predictable results by following ITIL® best practices and provides tooling and automation to increase efficiency and reduce your operational overhead and risk.
- https://aws.amazon.com/managed-services/#

ANALYTICS

Amazon Athena:

- Amazon Athena is an interactive query service that makes it easy to analyze data in Amazon S3 using standard SQL.
- Athena is serverless, so there is no infrastructure to manage. You pay only for the queries that you run.
- With a few clicks in the AWS Management Console, customers can point Athena at their data stored in S3 and begin using standard SQL to run ad-hoc queries and get results in seconds.
- You can use Athena to process logs, perform ad-hoc analysis and run interactive queries.
- Athena scales automatically – executing queries in parallel – so results are fast, even with large datasets and complex queries.
- https://aws.amazon.com/athena/features/

Amazon EMR:

- Amazon Elastic Map Reduce (EMR) provides a managed Hadoop framework that makes it easy, fast and cost-effective to process vast amounts of data across dynamically scalable Amazon EC2 instances.
- You can also run other popular distributed frameworks such as Apache Spark, HBase, Presto, and Flink in Amazon EMR and interact with data in other AWS data stores such as Amazon S3 and Amazon DynamoDB.
- Amazon EMR securely and reliably handles a broad set of big data use cases, including log analysis, web indexing, data transformations (ETL), machine learning, financial analysis, scientific simulation and bioinformatic.
- https://aws.amazon.com/emr/features/

Amazon CloudSearch:

- Amazon CloudSearch is a managed service in the AWS Cloud that makes it simple and cost-effective to set up, manage and scale a search solution for your website or application.
- Amazon CloudSearch supports 34 languages and popular search features such as highlighting, autocomplete and geospatial search.
- https://aws.amazon.com/cloudsearch/

Amazon Elasticsearch:

- Amazon Elasticsearch Service is a fully managed service that makes it easy for you to deploy, secure, operate and scale Elasticsearch to search, analyze and visualize data in real-time.

- With Amazon Elasticsearch Service, you get easy-to-use APIs and real-time analytics capabilities to power use-cases such as log analytics, full-text search, application monitoring and clickstream analytics, with enterprise-grade availability, scalability and security.

- https://aws.amazon.com/elasticsearch-service/features/

Amazon Kinesis:

- Amazon Kinesis makes it easy to collect, process and analyze real-time, streaming data so you can get timely insights and react quickly to new information.

- **There are four types of Kinesis service:**

    - Kinesis Video Streams makes it easy to securely stream video from connected devices to AWS for analytics, machine learning (ML), and other processing.

    - Kinesis Data Streams enables you to build custom applications that process or analyze streaming data for specialized needs.

    - Kinesis Data Firehose is the easiest way to load streaming data into data stores and analytics tools.

    - Amazon Kinesis Data Analytics is the easiest way to process and analyze real-time, streaming data.

- https://aws.amazon.com/kinesis/

- https://digitalcloud.training/certification-training/aws-solutions-architect-associate/analytics/amazon-kinesis/

AWS Data Pipeline:

- AWS Data Pipeline is a web service that helps you reliably process and move data between different AWS compute and storage services, as well as on-premises data sources at specified intervals.

- With AWS Data Pipeline, you can regularly access your data where it is stored, transform and process it at scale, and efficiently transfer the results to AWS services such as Amazon S3, Amazon RDS, Amazon DynamoDB and Amazon EMR.

- AWS Data Pipeline helps you easily create complex data processing workloads that are fault tolerant, repeatable and highly available.

- https://aws.amazon.com/datapipeline/

AWS Glue:

- AWS Glue is a fully managed extract, transform and load (ETL) service that makes it easy for customers to prepare and load their data for analytics.

- You can create and run an ETL job with a few clicks in the AWS Management Console.

- You simply point AWS Glue to your data stored on AWS, and AWS Glue discovers your data and stores the associated metadata (e.g., table definition and schema) in the AWS Glue Data Catalog.

- Once cataloged, your data is immediately searchable, queryable and available for ETL.

- AWS Glue generates the code to execute your data transformations and data loading processes.
- https://aws.amazon.com/glue/features/

MEDIA SERVICES

Amazon Elastic Transcoder:

- Amazon Elastic Transcoder is media transcoding in the cloud.
- It is designed to be a highly scalable, easy to use and a cost-effective way for developers and businesses to convert (or "transcode") media files from their source format into versions that will playback on devices like smartphones, tablets and PCs.
- https://aws.amazon.com/elastictranscoder/

SECURITY, IDENTITY AND COMPLIANCE

Amazon Cognito:

- Amazon Cognito lets you add user sign-up, sign-in and access control to your web and mobile apps quickly and easily.
- Amazon Cognito scales to millions of users and supports sign-in with social identity providers, such as Facebook, Google and Amazon, and enterprise identity providers via SAML 2.0.
- https://aws.amazon.com/cognito/details/

AWS Certificate Manager:

- AWS Certificate Manager is a service that lets you easily provision, manage and deploy public and private Secure Sockets Layer/Transport Layer Security (SSL/TLS) certificates for use with AWS services and your internal connected resources.
- SSL/TLS certificates are used to secure network communications and establish the identity of websites over the Internet as well as resources on private networks.
- AWS Certificate Manager removes the time-consuming manual process of purchasing, uploading and renewing SSL/TLS certificates.
- https://aws.amazon.com/certificate-manager/features/

AWS CloudHSM:

- AWS CloudHSM is a cloud-based hardware security module (HSM) that enables you to easily generate and use your own encryption keys on the AWS Cloud.
- With CloudHSM, you can manage your own encryption keys using FIPS 140-2 Level 3 validated HSMs.
- CloudHSM offers you the flexibility to integrate with your applications using industry-standard APIs, such as PKCS#11, Java Cryptography Extensions (JCE) and Microsoft CryptoNG (CNG) libraries.
- https://aws.amazon.com/cloudhsm/features/

AWS Directory Service:

- AWS Directory Service for Microsoft Active Directory, also known as AWS Managed Microsoft AD, enables your directory-aware workloads and AWS resources to use managed Active Directory in the AWS Cloud.

- AWS Managed Microsoft AD is built on actual Microsoft Active Directory and does not require you to synchronize or replicate data from your existing Active Directory to the cloud.

- You can use standard Active Directory administration tools and take advantage of built-in Active Directory features, such as Group Policy and single sign-on (SSO).

- With AWS Managed Microsoft AD, you can easily join Amazon EC2 and Amazon RDS for SQL Server instances to your domain, and use AWS Enterprise IT applications such as Amazon WorkSpaces with Active Directory users and groups.

- https://aws.amazon.com/directoryservice/features/

AWS Artifact:

- AWS Artifact is your go-to, central resource for compliance-related information that matters to you.

- It provides on-demand access to AWS' security and compliance reports and online agreements.

- Reports available in AWS Artifact include the Service Organization Control (SOC) reports, Payment Card Industry (PCI) reports, and certifications from accreditation bodies across geographies and compliance verticals that validate the implementation and operating effectiveness of AWS security controls.

- Agreements available in AWS Artifact include the Business Associate Addendum (BAA) and the Nondisclosure Agreement (NDA).

- https://aws.amazon.com/artifact/

MACHINE LEARNING

Amazon Rekognition:

- Amazon Rekognition makes it easy to add image and video analysis to your applications.

- You just provide an image or video to the Rekognition API, and the service can identify the objects, people, text, scenes and activities, as well as detect any inappropriate content.

- Amazon Rekognition also provides highly accurate facial analysis and facial recognition on images and video that you provide.

- You can detect, analyze and compare faces for a wide variety of user verification, people counting and public safety use cases.

- https://aws.amazon.com/rekognition/

Amazon SageMaker:

- Amazon SageMaker is a fully-managed platform that enables developers and data scientists to quickly and easily build, train and deploy machine learning models at any scale.

- Amazon SageMaker removes all the barriers that typically slow down developers who want to use machine learning.

- https://aws.amazon.com/sagemaker/features/

Amazon Comprehend:

- Amazon Comprehend is a natural language processing (NLP) service that uses machine learning to find insights and relationships in text.

- The service identifies the language of the text; extracts key phrases, places, people, brands, or events; understands how positive or negative the text is; analyzes text using tokenization and parts of speech; and automatically organizes a collection of text files by topic.

- Using these APIs, you can analyze text and apply the results in a wide range of applications including voice of customer analysis, intelligent document search and content personalization for web applications.

- https://aws.amazon.com/comprehend/features/

Amazon Transcribe:

- Amazon Transcribe is an automatic speech recognition (ASR) service that makes it easy for developers to add speech-to-text capability to their applications.

- Using the Amazon Transcribe API, you can analyze audio files stored in Amazon S3 and have the service return a text file of the transcribed speech.

- Amazon Transcribe can be used for lots of common applications, including the transcription of customer service calls and generating subtitles on audio and video content.

- The service can transcribe audio files stored in common formats, like WAV and MP3, with time stamps for every word so that you can easily locate the audio in the original source by searching for the text.

- https://aws.amazon.com/transcribe/

MOBILE SERVICES

AWS AppSync:

- AWS AppSync makes it easy to build data-driven mobile and browser-based apps that deliver responsive, collaborative experiences by keeping the data updated when devices are connected, enabling the app to use local data when offline, and synchronizing the data when the devices reconnect.

- AWS AppSync uses the open standard GraphQL query language so you can request, change and subscribe to the exact data you need with just a few lines of code.

- https://aws.amazon.com/appsync/product-details/

AWS Device Farm:

- AWS Device Farm is an app testing service that lets you test and interact with your Android, iOS and web apps on many devices at once, or reproduce issues on a device in real time.

- View video, screenshots, logs and performance data to pinpoint and fix issues and increase quality before shipping your app.

- https://aws.amazon.com/device-farm/

APPLICATION INTEGRATION

AWS Step Functions:

- AWS Step Functions lets you coordinate multiple AWS services into serverless workflows so you can build and update apps quickly.

- Using Step Functions, you can design and run workflows that stitch together services such as AWS Lambda and Amazon ECS into feature-rich applications.

- Workflows are made up of a series of steps, with the output of one step acting as input into the next.

- https://aws.amazon.com/step-functions/features/

Amazon MQ:

- Amazon MQ is a managed message broker service for Apache ActiveMQ that makes it easy to set up and operate message brokers in the cloud.

- Message brokers allow different software systems – often using different programming languages and on different platforms – to communicate and exchange information.

- Messaging is the communications backbone that connects and integrates the components of distributed applications, such as order processing, inventory management and order fulfillment for e-commerce.

- https://aws.amazon.com/amazon-mq/features/

Amazon SQS:

- Amazon Simple Queue Service (SQS) is a fully managed message queuing service that enables you to decouple and scale microservices, distributed systems and serverless applications.

- SQS eliminates the complexity and overhead associated with managing and operating message-oriented middleware. It empowers developers to focus on differentiating work.

- Using SQS, you can send, store and receive messages between software components at any volume, without losing messages or requiring other services to be available.

- https://aws.amazon.com/sqs/features/

Amazon SWF:

- Amazon SWF helps developers build, run and scale background jobs that have parallel or sequential steps.

- You can think of Amazon SWF as a fully-managed state tracker and task coordinator in the Cloud.

- https://aws.amazon.com/swf/

INTERNET OF THINGS

AWS IoT Core:

- AWS IoT Core is a managed cloud service that lets connected devices easily and securely interact with cloud applications and other devices.

- AWS IoT Core can support billions of devices and trillions of messages and can process and route those messages to AWS endpoints and to other devices reliably and securely.

- With AWS IoT Core, your applications can keep track of and communicate with all your devices, all the time, even when they aren't connected.

- https://aws.amazon.com/iot-core/features/

DESKTOP & APP STREAMING

Amazon Workspaces:

- Amazon WorkSpaces is a managed, secure cloud desktop service. You can use Amazon WorkSpaces to provision either Windows or Linux desktops in just a few minutes and quickly scale to provide thousands of desktops to workers across the globe.

- Amazon WorkSpaces offers you an easy way to provide a secure, managed, cloud-based virtual desktop experience to your end-users.

- Unlike traditional on-premises Virtual Desktop Infrastructure (VDI) solutions, you don't have to worry about procuring, deploying and managing a complex environment – Amazon WorkSpaces takes care of the heavy lifting and provides a fully managed service.

- https://aws.amazon.com/workspaces/features/

AWS ANALYTICS

The are several AWS Analytics services and these include:

- Amazon Athena   *interactive query service*
- Amazon EMR   *Elastic Map Reduce*
- Amazon CloudSearch   *like Google search for websites*
- Amazon Elasticsearch Service
- Amazon Kinesis   *Streaming data*
- Amazon QuickSight
- Amazon Data Pipeline   *to process and move data*
- AWS Glue   *discovers data and then stores metadata*
- AWS Lake Formation
- Amazon MSK

In this section, we will focus on Athena, EMR, Glue and Kinesis as these are the services that are most likely to come up on the AWS Certified Cloud Practitioner exam. You may also want to read about the other services mentioned above to understand what they are about at a high-level.

AMAZON ELASTIC MAP REDUCE

Amazon EMR is a web service that enables businesses, researchers, data analysts and developers to easily and cost-effectively process vast amounts of data.

EMR utilizes a hosted Hadoop framework running on Amazon EC2 and Amazon S3.

Managed Hadoop framework for processing huge amounts of data.

Apache Spark, HBase, Presto and Flink are also supported.

Most commonly used for log analysis, financial analysis or extract, translate and loading (ETL) activities.

A Step is a programmatic task for performing some process on the data (e.g., count words).

A cluster is a collection of EC2 instances provisioned by EMR to run your Steps.

EMR uses Apache Hadoop as its distributed data processing engine: an open source and Java software framework that supports data-intensive distributed applications running on large clusters of commodity hardware.

EMR is a good place to deploy Apache Spark, an open-source distributed processing used for big data workloads which utilizes in-memory caching and optimized query execution.

You can also launch Presto clusters. Presto is an open-source distributed SQL query engine designed for fast analytic queries against large datasets.

EMR launches all nodes for a given cluster in the same Amazon EC2 Availability Zone.

You can access Amazon EMR by using the AWS Management Console, Command Line Tools, SDKS or the EMR API.

With EMR you have access to the underlying operating system (you can SSH in).

AMAZON ATHENA

Amazon Athena is an interactive query service that makes it easy to analyze data in Amazon S3 using standard SQL.

Athena is serverless, so there is no infrastructure to manage, and you pay only for the queries that you run.

Athena is easy to use – simply point to your data in Amazon S3, define the schema and start querying using standard SQL.

Amazon Athena uses Presto with full standard SQL support, and works with a variety of standard data formats, including CSV, JSON, ORC, Apache Parquet and Avro.

While Amazon Athena is ideal for quick, ad-hoc querying and integrates with Amazon QuickSight for easy visualization, it can also handle complex analysis, including large joins, window functions and arrays.

Amazon Athena uses a managed Data Catalog to store information and schemas about the databases and tables that you create for your data stored in Amazon S3.

AWS GLUE

AWS Glue is a fully-managed, pay-as-you-go, extract, transform and load (ETL) service that automates the time-consuming steps of data preparation for analytics.

AWS Glue automatically discovers and profiles data via the Glue Data Catalog, recommends and generates ETL code to transform your source data into target schemas.

AWS Glue runs the ETL jobs on a fully managed, scale-out Apache Spark environment to load your data into its destination.

AWS Glue also allows you to setup, orchestrate and monitor complex data flows.

You can create and run an ETL job with a few clicks in the AWS Management Console.

Use AWS Glue to discover properties of data, transform it and prepare it for analytics.

Glue can automatically discover both structured and semi-structured data stored in data lakes on Amazon S3, data warehouses in Amazon Redshift and various databases running on AWS.

It provides a unified view of data via the Glue Data Catalog that is available for ETL, querying and reporting using services like Amazon Athena, Amazon EMR, and Amazon Redshift Spectrum.

Glue automatically generates Scala or Python code for ETL jobs that you can further customize using tools you are already familiar with.

AWS Glue is serverless, so there are no compute resources to configure and manage.

DATA ANALYSIS AND QUERY USE CASES

Query services like Amazon Athena, data warehouses like Amazon Redshift and sophisticated data processing frameworks like Amazon EMR, all address different needs and use cases.

Amazon Redshift provides the fastest query performance for enterprise reporting and business intelligence workloads, particularly those involving extremely complex SQL with multiple joins and sub-queries.

Amazon EMR makes it simple and cost effective to run highly distributed processing frameworks such as Hadoop, Spark and Presto when compared to on-premises deployments. Amazon EMR is flexible – you can run custom applications and code, and define specific compute, memory, storage and application parameters to optimize your analytic requirements.

Amazon Athena provides the easiest way to run ad-hoc queries for data in S3 without the need to setup or manage any servers.

The table below shows the primary use case and situations for using a few AWS query and analytics services:

AWS Service	Primary Use Case	When to use
Amazon Athena	Query	Run interactive queries against data directly in Amazon S3 without worrying about formatting data or managing infrastructure. Can use with other services such as Amazon RedShift
Amazon RedShift	Data Warehouse	Pull data from many sources, format and organize it, store it, and support complex, high speed queries that produce business reports.
Amazon EMR	Data Processing	Highly distributed processing frameworks such as Hadoop, Spark, and Presto. Run a wide variety of scale-out data processing tasks for applications such as machine learning, graph analytics, data transformation, streaming data.
AWS Glue	ETL Service *Extract Transform Load*	Transform and move data to various destinations. Used to prepare and load data for analytics. Data source can be S3, RedShift or other database Glue Data Catalog can be queried by Athena, EMR and RedShift Spectrum

AMAZON KINESIS

Amazon Kinesis makes it easy to collect, process and analyze real-time, streaming data so you can get timely insights and react quickly to new information.

Collection of services for processing streams of various data.

Data is processed in "shards".

There are **four types of Kinesis service** and these are detailed below.

Kinesis Video Streams

Kinesis Video Streams makes it easy to securely stream video from connected devices to AWS for analytics, machine learning (ML) and other processing.

Durably stores, encrypts and indexes video data streams, and allows access to data through easy-to-use APIs.

Producers provide data streams.

Stores data for 24 hours by default, up to 7 days.

Consumers receive and process data.

Can have multiple shards in a stream.

Supports encryption at rest with server-side encryption (KMS) with a customer master key.

Kinesis Data Streams

Kinesis Data Streams enables you to build custom applications that process or analyze streaming data for specialized needs.

Kinesis Data Streams enables real-time processing of streaming big data.

Kinesis Data Streams is useful for rapidly moving data off data producers and then continuously processing the data.

Kinesis Data Streams **stores data** for later processing by applications (key difference with Firehose which delivers data directly to AWS services).

Common use cases include:

- Accelerated log and data feed intake
- Real-time metrics and reporting
- Real-time data analytics
- Complex stream processing

Kinesis Data Firehose

Kinesis Data Firehose is the easiest way to load streaming data into data stores and analytics tools.

Captures, transforms and loads streaming data.

Enables near real-time analytics with existing business intelligence tools and dashboards.

Kinesis Data Streams can be used as the source(s) to Kinesis Data Firehose.

You can configure Kinesis Data Firehose to transform your data before delivering it.

With Kinesis Data Firehose, you don't need to write an application or manage resources.

Firehose can batch, compress and encrypt data before loading it.

Firehose synchronously replicates data across three AZs as it is transported to destinations.

Each delivery stream stores data records for up to 24 hours.

Kinesis Data Analytics

Amazon Kinesis Data Analytics is the easiest way to process and analyze real-time, streaming data.

Can use standard SQL queries to process Kinesis data streams.

Provides real-time analysis.

Use cases:

- Generate time-series analytics
- Feed real-time dashboards
- Create real-time alerts and notifications

Quickly author and run powerful SQL code against streaming sources.

Can ingest data from Kinesis Streams and Kinesis Firehose.

Output to S3, RedShift, Elasticsearch and Kinesis Data Streams.

Sits over Kinesis Data Streams and Kinesis Data Firehose.

CONCLUSION

We trust that these training notes have helped you to gain a complete understanding of the facts you need to know to pass the AWS Certified Cloud Practitioner exam first time.

The exam covers a broad set of technologies. It's vital to ensure you are armed with the knowledge to answer whatever questions come up in your certification exam. We therefore recommend reviewing these training notes until you're confident in all areas.

BEFORE TAKING THE AWS EXAM

Familiarize yourself with the AWS platform

If you're new to Cloud Computing, it's highly advisable to take the instructor-led video course from Digital Cloud Training for a more detailed understanding of the AWS services before sitting your exam. With over 12 hours of video lessons, this on-demand video course will maximize your chances of passing your exam first time with a great score.

Assess your exam readiness with practice exams from Digital Cloud Training

These popular practice tests are the closest to the actual exam question format and the only exam-difficulty questions on the market. If you can pass these mock exams, you're well set to ace the real thing!

To learn more, visit https://digitalcloud.training/aws-certified-cloud-practitioner-training-course.

Apply coupon code **AMZ20** at checkout for a **20% discount**.

REACH OUT AND CONNECT

We want you to have a 5-star learning experience. If anything is not 100% to your liking, please email us at support@digitalcloud.training. We promise to address all questions and concerns. We really want you to get great value from these training resources.

The AWS platform is evolving quickly, and the exam tracks these changes with a typical lag of around 6 months. We are therefore reliant on student feedback to keep track of what is appearing in the exam. If there are any topics in your exam that weren't covered in our training resources, please provide us with feedback using this form https://digitalcloud.training/student-feedback. We appreciate your feedback that will help us further improve our AWS training resources.

To discuss any exam-specific questions you may have, please join the discussion on Slack. Visit http://digitalcloud.training/slack for instructions.

Also, remember to join our private Facebook group to ask questions and share your knowledge with the AWS community: https://www.facebook.com/groups/awscertificationqa

BONUS OFFER

To gain access to your free practice exam with **65 exam-difficulty questions** on the interactive online exam simulator, visit https://digitalcloud.training/free-aws-practice-questions-cloud-practitioner/ or simply scan this QR code.

For those who have already purchased the full set of practice questions, please note that the questions are included in the pool of 500 questions.

LEAVE US A REVIEW

If you like reading course reviews, please consider paying it forward. Your reviews help us improve our courses and help your fellow AWS students make the right choices. We celebrate every honest review and truly appreciate it. You can leave a review at any time by visiting amazon.com/ryp or your local amazon store (e.g. amazon.co.uk/ryp).

Best wishes for your AWS certification journey!

OTHER BOOKS & COURSES BY NEAL DAVIS

All of our courses are available on **digitalcloud.training/aws-training-courses**

Apply coupon code **AMZ20** for a 20% discount.

COURSES FOR THE AWS CERTIFIED CLOUD PRACTITIONER

Course	Description
AWS Certified Cloud Practitioner Instructor-led Video Course	**HIGHLY FLEXIBLE COURSE STRUCTURE:** You can move quickly through the course, focusing on the theory lectures. **GUIDED HANDS-ON EXERCISES:** To gain more practical experience with AWS services, you have the option to explore the guided hands-on exercises. **EXAM-CRAM LECTURES**: Get through the key exam facts in the shortest time possible with the exam-cram lectures that you'll find at the end of each section. **HIGH-QUALITY VISUALS**: We've spared no effort to create a highly visual training course with lots of table and graphs.
AWS Certified Cloud Practitioner (online) Practice Exams + Exam Simulator	Get access to the **Practice Exam course** from Digital Cloud Training: 6 sets of practice tests with 65 Questions each. All questions are unique, 100% scenario-based and conform to the latest CLF-C01 exam blueprint. Our AWS Practice Tests are delivered in 4 different modes: • Exam Mode • Training Mode • Knowledge Reviews • Final Exam Simulator (with 500 practice questions)

AWS Certified Cloud Practitioner (offline) Practice Tests (ebook)	There are **6 practice exams with 65 questions each** covering the five domains of the AWS CLF-C01 exam blueprint. Each set of questions is repeated once without answers and explanations, and once with answers and explanations, so you get to choose from two methods of preparation: 1: To simulate the exam experience and assess your exam readiness, use the "**PRACTICE QUESTIONS ONLY**" sets. 2: To use the practice questions as a learning tool, use the "**PRACTICE QUESTIONS, ANSWERS & EXPLANATIONS**" sets to view the answers and read the in-depth explanations as you move through the questions.
Training Notes for the AWS Certified Cloud Practitioner (cheat sheets)	This book is based on the CLF-C01 exam blueprint and provides a deep dive into the subject matter in a concise and easy-to-read format so you can fast-track your time to success. AWS Solutions Architect, Neal Davis, has consolidated the information you need to be successful.

COURSES FOR THE AWS CERTIFIED SOLUTIONS ARCHITECT ASSOCIATE

Course	Description
AWS Certified Solutions Architect Associate Instructor-led Video Course	This popular AWS Certified Solutions Architect Associate (SAA-C02) video course is delivered through guided Hands-On Labs exercises • 28 hours Video Lessons • Exam Cram Lectures • 90 Quiz Questions • Guided Hands-on Exercises
AWS Certified Solutions Architect Associate (online) Practice Tests	Get access to the **Practice Exam course** from Digital Cloud Training: 6 sets of practice tests with 65 Questions each. All questions are unique, 100% scenario-based and conform to the latest AWS SAA-C02 exam blueprint. Our AWS Practice Tests are delivered in 4 different modes: • Exam Mode • Training Mode

	- Knowledge Reviews - Final Exam Simulator (with 500 practice questions)
AWS Certified Solutions Architect Associate (offline) Practice Tests (ebook)	There are **6 practice exams with 65 questions each** covering the AWS SAA-C02 exam blueprint. Each set of questions is repeated once without answers and explanations, and once with answers and explanations. 1: To simulate the exam experience and assess your exam readiness, use the "**PRACTICE QUESTIONS ONLY**" sets. 2: To use the practice questions as a learning tool, use the "**PRACTICE QUESTIONS, ANSWERS & EXPLANATIONS**" sets to view the answers and read the in-depth explanations as you move through the questions.
Training Notes for the AWS Certified Solutions Architect Associate (cheat sheets)	Deep dive into the SAA-C02 exam objectives with over 300 pages of detailed facts, tables and diagrams. Save valuable time by getting straight to the facts you need to know to pass your AWS Certified Solutions Architect Associate exam first time! This book is based on the 2020 SAA-C02 exam blueprint and provides a deep dive into the subject matter in a concise and easy-to-read format so you can fast-track your time to success.

COURSES FOR THE AWS CERTIFIED DEVELOPER ASSOCIATE

Course	Description
AWS Certified Developer Associate Instructor led Video Course	This popular **AWS Certified Developer Associate Exam Training** for the **DVA-C01 certification exam** is packed with over 28 hours of comprehensive video lessons, hands-on labs, quizzes and exam-crams. With our mixture of in-depth theory, architectural diagrams and hands-on training, you'll learn how to architect and build applications on **Amazon Web Services**, fully preparing you for the **AWS Developer Certification** exam. With this complete **AWS Developer training** course, you have everything you need to comfortably pass the **AWS Developer Certification** exam at the first attempt.
AWS Certified Developer Associate (online) Practice Tests	Get access to the **Practice Exam Course** from Digital Cloud Training with 390 Questions in 6 sets of practice tests. All questions are unique and conform to the latest AWS DVA-C01 exam blueprint. Our AWS Practice Tests are delivered in 4 different modes: - Exam Mode

	• Training Mode
	• Knowledge Reviews
	• Final Exam Simulator
AWS Certified Developer Associate (offline) Practice Tests (ebook)	There are **6 practice exams with 65 questions each** covering all topics for the AWS DVA-C01 exam. Each set of questions is repeated once without answers and explanations, and once with answers and explanations, so you get to choose from two methods of preparation: 1: To simulate the exam experience and assess your exam readiness, use the "**PRACTICE QUESTIONS ONLY**" sets. 2: To use the practice questions as a learning tool, use the "**PRACTICE QUESTIONS, ANSWERS & EXPLANATIONS**" sets to view the answers and read the in-depth explanations as you move through the questions.
Training Notes for the AWS Certified Developer Associate (cheat sheets)	With these in-depth AWS Training Notes for the Developer Associate, you'll learn everything you need to know to ace your exam! Fast-track your exam success with over 340 pages of exam-specific facts, tables and diagrams. AWS Solution Architect and founder of Digital Cloud Training, Neal Davis, has consolidated ALL of the key information into this essential cheat sheet. Based on the latest DVA-C01 certification exam, these Training Notes will shortcut your study time and maximize your chance of passing your exam first time.

COURSES FOR THE AWS CERTIFIED SYSOPS ADMINISTRATOR ASSOCIATE

Course	Description
AWS Certified SysOps Administrator Associate Instructor led Video Course	This popular **AWS Certified SysOps Administrator Exam Training** for the **SOA-C01 certification exam** is packed with 15 hours of comprehensive video lessons, exam scenarios and practical exercises. With our mixture of in-depth theory, logical diagrams and hands-on training, you'll learn how deploy, manage, and operate scalable, highly available, and fault tolerant systems on AWS, fully preparing you for the AWS SysOps Certification exam. With this complete **AWS SysOps training** course, you have everything you need to comfortably pass the **AWS SysOps Certification** exam at the first attempt.
AWS Certified SysOps Administrator Associate (online) Practice Tests	Get access to the **Practice Exam Course** from Digital Cloud Training with 195 Questions in 3 sets of practice tests. All questions are unique and conform to the latest AWS SOA-C01 exam blueprint.

	Our AWS Practice Tests are delivered in 4 different modes: • Exam Mode • Training Mode • Knowledge Reviews • Final Exam Simulator
Training Notes for the AWS Certified SysOps Administrator Associate (cheat sheets)	With these in-depth AWS Training Notes for the SysOps Administrator, you'll learn everything you need to know to ace your exam! Fast-track your exam success with exam-specific facts, tables and diagrams. Founder of Digital Cloud Training, Neal Davis, has consolidated ALL of the key information into this essential cheat sheet. Based on the latest SOA-C01 certification exam, these Training Notes will shortcut your study time and maximize your chance of passing your exam first time.

ABOUT THE AUTHOR

Neal Davis is the founder of Digital Cloud Training, AWS Cloud Solutions Architect and successful IT instructor. With more than 20 years of experience in the tech industry, Neal is a true expert in virtualization and cloud computing. His passion is to help others achieve career success by offering in-depth AWS certification training resources.

Neal started **Digital Cloud Training** to provide a variety of training resources for Amazon Web Services (AWS) certifications that represent a higher standard of quality than is otherwise available in the market.

Through our hands-on AWS training courses, we help students build the knowledge and practical skill set they need to not only pass their AWS certification exams with flying colors but to also excel in their cloud career.

Our AWS training is delivered to suit many learning styles, using an effective combination of visual aids, hands-on training, online cheat sheets and high quality practice questions that reflect the difficulty and style of real AWS exam questions.

With all of these quality resources, learners have everything they need to confidently pass their exams. Students regularly report pass marks with average scores well above 85%.

We've built an active community around our cutting-edge training courses so you have the guidance and support you need every step of the way. Join the AWS Community of over 250,000 happy students that are currently enrolled in Digital Cloud Training courses.

CONNECT WITH NEAL ON SOCIAL MEDIA

All Links available on https://digitalcloud.training/neal-davis

 digitalcloud.training/neal-davis

 youtube.com/c/digitalcloudtraining

 facebook.com/digitalcloudtraining

 Twitter @nealkdavis

 linkedin.com/in/nealkdavis

 Instagram @digitalcloudtraining

Made in the USA
Middletown, DE
25 May 2021